3rd Workshop on Sentiment Analysis where AI meets Psychology

(SAAIP 2013)

Held at the 6th International Joint Conference on Natural Language Processing (IJCNLP 2013)

Nagoya, Japan
14-18 October 2013

ISBN: 978-1-62993-541-6

Printed from e-media with permission by:

Curran Associates, Inc.
57 Morehouse Lane
Red Hook, NY 12571

Some format issues inherent in the e-media version may also appear in this print version.

Printed by Curran Associates, Inc. (2014)

For permission requests, please contact the Association for Computational Linguistics at the address below.

Association for Computational Linguistics
209 N. Eighth Street
Stroudsburg, Pennsylvania 18360

Phone: 1-570-476-8006
Fax: 1-570-476-0860

acl@aclweb.org

Additional copies of this publication are available from:

Curran Associates, Inc.
57 Morehouse Lane
Red Hook, NY 12571 USA
Phone: 845-758-0400
Fax: 845-758-2634
Email: curran@proceedings.com
Web: www.proceedings.com

Table of Contents

Sixth International Joint Conference on
Natural Language Processing

IJCNLP2013
THE 6TH INTERNATIONAL JOINT CONFERENCE ON
NATURAL LANGUAGE PROCESSING
OCTOBER 14–18, 2013
NAGOYA CONGRESS CENTER, NAGOYA, JAPAN

Proceedings of the 3rd Workshop on Sentiment Analysis where AI meets Psychology (SAAIP 2013)

Preface

In recent times, research activities in the areas of Opinion, Sentiment and/or Emotion in natural language texts and other media are gaining ground under the umbrella of affect computing. Huge amount of text data are available in the Social Web in the form of news, reviews, blogs, chats and even twitter. Sentiment analysis from natural language text is a multifaceted and multidisciplinary problem. The existing reported solutions or available systems are still far from perfect or fail to meet the satisfaction level of the end users. There are many conceptual rules that govern sentiment and there are even more clues (possibly unlimited) that can map these concepts from realization to verbalization of a human being. Human psychology that relates to social, cultural, behavioral and environmental aspects of civilization may provide the unrevealed clues and govern the sentiment realization. In the present scenario we need constant research endeavors to reveal and incorporate the human psychological knowledge into machines in the best possible ways. The important issues that need attention include how various psychological phenomena can be explained in computational terms and the various artificial intelligence (AI) concepts and computer modeling methodologies that are most useful from the psychologist's point of view.

Regular research papers on sentiment analysis continue to be published in reputed conferences like ACL, EACL, NAACL, EMNLP or COLING. The Sentiment Analysis Symposiums are also drawing the attention of the research communities from every nook and corner of the world. There have been an increasing number of efforts in shared tasks such as SemEval 2007 Task 14: Affective Text, SemEval 2013 Task 14: Sentiment Analysis on Twitter, TAC 2008 Opinion Summarization task, TREC-BLOG tracks since 2006 and relevant NTCIR tracks since 6th NTCIR that have aimed to focus on different issues of opinion and emotion analysis. Several communities from sentiment analysis have engaged themselves to conduct relevant conferences, e.g., Affective Computing and Intelligent Interfaces (ACII) in 2009, 2011 and 2013 and workshops such as Sentiment and Subjectivity in Text in COLING - ACL 2006, Sentiment Analysis – Emotion, Metaphor, Ontology and Terminology (EMOT) in LREC 2008, Opinion Mining and Sentiment Analysis (WOMSA) 2009, Topic - Sentiment Analysis for Mass Opinion Measurement (TSA) in CIKM 2009, Computational Approaches to Analysis and Generation of Emotion in Text in NAACL 2010, Workshop on Computational Approaches to Subjectivity and Sentiment Analysis (WASSA) in ECAI 2010, ACL 2011, ACL 2012 and NAACL-HLT 2013, FLAIRS 2011 special track on Affect Computing, Sentiment Elicitation from Natural Text for Information Retrieval and Extraction (SENTIRE 2011 and SENTIRE 2012), EMOTION SENTIMENT and SOCIAL SIGNALS (ES3 2012) in the satellite of LREC 2012, Practice and Theory of Opinion Mining and Sentiment Analysis in conjunction with KONVENS - 2012 (PATHOS 2012, 2013), Workshop on Intelligent Approaches applied to Sentiment Mining and Emotion Analysis (WISMEA 2012), Workshop on Issues of Sentiment Discovery and Opinion Mining (WISDOM 2012, 2013) and a bunch of special sessions like Sentiment Analysis for Asian Languages (SAAL, 2012), Brain Inspired Natural Language Processing (BINLP 2012), Advances in Cognitive and Emotional Information Processing (ACEIP, 2012) and so on.

Since our previous two workshops in conjunction with the International Joint Conference on NLP (IJCNLP) in Chiang Mai, Thailand during Nov. 7-13, 2011 and with the International Conference on Computational Linguistics (COLING) in Mumbai, India during Dec. 8-15, 2012 were quite successful (with 20 and 14 submissions and more than 30 participants from many countries), we are planning to conduct our next workshop in conjunction with the International Joint Conference on NLP (IJCNLP) in Nagoya, Japan during Oct. 14-18, 2013. Inspired by the objectives we aimed at in the first two editions of the workshop, the warm responses and feedbacks we received from the participants and attendees and the final outcome, the purpose of the proposed 3rd edition of the Workshop on Sentiment Analysis where AI meets Psychology (SAAIP 2013) is to create a framework for presenting and discussing the challenges related to sentiment, opinion and emotion analysis in the ground of NLP. This workshop also aims to bring together the researchers in multiple disciplines such as computer science, psychology, cognitive science, social science and many more who are interested in developing next generation machines that can recognize and respond to the sentimental states of the human users. This time we received only nine submissions and finally four papers have been accepted. Increasing number of workshops in similar field day-by-day may be one of the reasons for less number of submissions this time.

The lexical based polarity classification used in sentiment analysis achieved relatively good results in Czech, still classifier shows some error rate. Kateřina Veselovská and Jan Hajič, jr. provided a detailed analysis of such errors caused both by the system and by human reviewers. They have analyzed different types of classifier errors on the real evaluative data and have suggested various improvements. Yasuhide Miura, Keigo Hattori, Tomoko Ohkuma and Hiroshi Masuichi proposed a method to extract sentiment topics from a Japanese text. They utilized sentiment clues and a relaxed labeling schema to extract sentiment topics.

Nataliya Panasenko, Andrej Trnka, Dana Petranová and Slavomír Magál presented the results of GRID project which aimed at studying the semantics of 24 emotion terms in 23 languages belonging to 8 language families (Indo-European, Indo-Iranian, Afro-Asiatic, Altaic, Uralic, Japonic, Sino-Tibetan, Niger-Congo, and Unclassified). They processed large volume of information from about 5000 active project participants who live in 30 countries. The work has been carried out on two Slavic languages – Slovak and Czech and on two emotion terms – love and hatred.

Not only text, music is also a universal language to convey sentiments. Less attention has been paid to the emotion recognition in Indian songs to date. Braja Gopal Patra, Dipankar Das and Sivaji Bandyopadhyay have built a system for classifying moods of Hindi songs using different audio related features like rhythm, timber and intensity on a small dataset of 230 songs.

We thank all the members of the Program Committee for their excellent and insightful reviews, the authors who submitted contributions for the workshop and the participants for making the workshop a success. We also express our thanks to the IJCNLP 2013 Organizing Committee and Local Organizing Committee for their support and cooperation in organizing the workshop.

Organizing Committee
3rd Workshop on Sentiment Analysis where AI meets Psychology
IJCNLP 2013
October 14, 2013

Organizers:

Sivaji Bandyopadhyay, Jadavpur University, Kolkata (India) (Organizing Chair)
Manabu Okumurra, Tokyo Institute of Technology, Tokyo (Japan) (Organizing Chair)
Braja Gopal Patra, Jadavpur University (India)

Program Committee:

Khurshid Ahmad, Trinity College Dublin (Ireland)
Alexandra Balahur, European Commission Joint Research Centre - Ispra (Italy)
Erik Cambria, National University of Singapore(Singapore)
Amitava Das, University of North Texas (USA)
Dipankar Das, National Institute of Technology (NIT), Meghalaya(India)
Diana Inkpen, University of Ottawa (Canada)
Noriko Kando, National Institute of Informatics (Japan)
Alena Neviarouskaya, University of Tokyo (Japan)
Vincent Ng, University of Texas at Dallas, (USA)
Fuji Ren, University of Tokushima (Japan)
Paolo Rosso, Universitat Politecnica de Valencia (Spain)
Patrick Saint-Dizier, IRIT-CNRS (France)
Swapna Somasundaran, Siemens Corporate Research (SCR)(USA)
Veselin Stoyanov, Cornell University (USA)
Carlo Strapparava, Fondazione Bruno Kessler (FBK), (Italy)
Stan Szpakowicz, University of Ottawa (Canada)
Theresa Wilson, University of Edinburgh (UK)
Michael Zock, LIF-CNRS, Marseille (France)
Alessandro Valitutti, University of Helsinki (Finland)
Veronica Perez-Rosas, University of North Texas (USA)
Alexander Gelbukh, Center for Computing Research, CIC (Mexico)
Adam Bermingham, Dublin City University (Ireland)

Workshop Program

Monday, October 14, 2013

09:30–09:45 Opening Remarks

Session 1:

09:45–10:15 *Why Words Alone Are Not Enough: Error Analysis of Lexicon-based Polarity Classifier for Czech*
Kateřina Veselovská and Jan Hajič, jr.

10:15–10:45 *Topic Modeling with Sentiment Clues and Relaxed Labeling Schema*
Yasuhide Miura, Keigo Hattori, Tomoko Ohkuma and Hiroshi Masuichi

10:45–11:15 *Bilingual analysis of LOVE and HATRED emotional markers (SPSS-based approach)*
Nataliya Panasenko, Andrej Trnka, Dana Petranová and Slavomír Magál

11:15–11:45 *Automatic Music Mood Classification of Hindi Songs*
Braja Gopal Patra, Dipankar Das and Sivaji Bandyopadhyay

We wish to thank our sponsors and supporters!

Platinum Sponsors

NLP

www.anlp.jp

Silver Sponsors

Google™

www.google.com

Bronze Sponsors

Rakuten

www.rakuten.com

Supporters

NAGOYA CONVENTION
& VISITORS BUREAU

Nagoya Convention & Visitors Bureau

We wish to thank our organizers!

Organizers

Asian Federation of Natural Language Processing (AFNLP)

Toyohashi University of Technology

Why Words Alone Are Not Enough: Error Analysis of Lexicon-based Polarity Classifier for Czech

Kateřina Veselovská
Charles University in Prague
Faculty of Mathematics and Physics
Institute of Formal and Applied Linguistics
veselovska@ufal.mff.cuni.cz

Jan Hajič, jr.
Charles University in Prague
Faculty of Mathematics and Physics
Institute of Formal and Applied Linguistics
hajicj@ufal.mff.cuni.cz

Abstract

Lexicon-based classifier is in the long term one of the main and most effective methods of polarity classification used in sentiment analysis, i.e. computational study of opinions, sentiments and emotions expressed in text (see Liu, 2010). Although it achieves relatively good results also for Czech, the classifier still shows some error rate. This paper provides a detailed analysis of such errors caused both by the system and by human reviewers. The identified errors are representatives of the challenges faced by the entire area of opinion mining. Therefore, the analysis is essential for further research in the field and serves as a basis for meaningful improvements of the system.

1 Introduction

After finishing the initial phase of our research in the area of sentiment analysis in Czech during which the collected data resources were manually annotated, we attempted to train two classifiers for automatic polarity detection of a given text: the lexicon-based classifier and the Naive Bayes classifier. Both systems were trained on two different types of the data (see Section 3). As shown in Table 1, the Naive Bayes classifier was consistently outperformed by the primary lexicon-based one (denoted as PC in the table), which on the less complicated data performed comparably to state-of-the-art, see Cui et al. (2006). Acc, R, P and F stand for accuracy, recall, precision and F-measure, respectively.

Model	Acc	R(-)	P(-)	F(-)	R(+)	P(+)	F(+)	R	P	F
baseline	0.630	0	0	0	1	0.630	0.773	0.370	0.233	0.286
PC, train	0.960	0.964	0.935	0.949	0.958	0.977	0.967	0.960	0.961	0.960
PC, test	0.889	0.907	0.821	0.862	0.878	0.939	0.908	0.889	0.894	0.890
Bayes,train	0.864	0.717	0.901	0.798	0.955	0.849	0.899	0.803	0.879	0.833
Bayes, test	0.827	0.630	0.872	0.730	0.947	0.811	0.874	0.745	0.847	0.781

Table 1. Baseline, comparing performance on training and test data

We will briefly describe the system below in Section 4. The results are discussed in detail in Veselovská (2012).

2 Related Work

The very first stage of the project has been described in Veselovská et al. (2012). Closely related work using methods that analyze sentiment on a deep level is done by Polanyi and Zaenen (2004), who consider the role of lexical and discourse context of the attitudinal sentences. The importance of discourse, namely interaction between opinions, is also emphasized by Johansson and Moschitti (2013), who demonstrate that relational features, mainly derived from dependency-syntactic and semantic role structures, can significantly improve the performance of automatic systems for a number of fine-grained opinion analysis tasks. There is a number of papers dealing with sentiment analysis from the point of view of compositional semantics. Whereas Choi and Cardie (2008) show that simple heuristics based on compositional semantics can perform better than learning-based methods that do not incorporate compositional semantics, Moilanen and Pulman (2007) explain sentiment classification of grammatical constituents in quasi-

Proceedings of the 3rd Workshop on Sentiment Analysis where AI meets Psychology (SAAIP 2013), IJCNLP 2013, pages 1–5, Nagoya, Japan, October 14, 2013.

compositional way. Some work on sentiment analysis in Czech has been also done by Habernal et al. (2013), but so far no authors provided error analysis of Czech polarity classifiers.

3 Data

Since our initial motivation was to create a tool for detecting the way news articles might influence public opinion, we firstly worked with the data obtained from the Home section of the Czech news website Aktualne.cz (*http://aktualne.centrum.cz/*) – or more precisely, with the articles primarily concerned with domestic politics, namely the situation before the elections in 2010. Unfortunately, it turned out that the analysis of such texts was a rather difficult task in terms of automatic processing, because Czech journalists mostly avoid strongly evaluative expressions. Moreover, the corpus was not large enough for a full-scale evaluation, as it contained merely 410 segments of texts (6,868 words, 1,935 unique lemmas) which were manually annotated on polarity. Also, the language we were dealing with was not straightforward. Furthermore, the distribution of polarity classes over segments was very nonuniform, with neutral segments occupying 78% of the data and positive segments making up less than 5%. Given the small size of the data, it was practically unachievable to correctly classify positive segments, and those that were classified correctly were usually swamped by positively classified neutral segments. The same problem appeared in case of negative segments, although less severe. Consequently, it was not possible to provide the error analysis based on the results from Aktualne.cz data.

Therefore, we decided to use the auxiliary data: the domestic appliance reviews from the Mall.cz (*http://www.mall.cz/*) retail server obtained from a private company. The Mall.cz corpus is much bigger (158,955 words, 13,473 lemmas). These reviews were divided into positive (6,365) and negative (3,812) by their authors. We found this data much easier to work with, because they are primarily evaluative by their nature and contain no complicated syntactic or semantic structures. Unlike the data from Aktualne.cz, they also contain explicit polar expressions in a prototypical use. Furthermore, they do not need to be tagged for the gold-standard annotation. The Mall.cz data, however, do present a different set of complications: the grammatical mistakes or typing errors cause noise in the form of additional lemmas and some of the reviews are also categorized incorrectly. However, compared to the problems with the news articles, these are only minor difficulties which can be easily solved. For this reason, the Mall.cz data are more suitable for the error analysis task.

4 The Lexicon-based Classifier System

There are several steps leading to the effective lexicon-based classifier. During the preprocessing phase, all the data first undergo lemmatization, using a tagger of Hajič (2004). From the tagger output, not only do we retain the lemma but also the part of speech and negation morphological tags. Then, we automatically generate a polarity lexicon from the training data and compute the measurement of how reliable a given lexicon item works as a polarity indicator. From our data, we first need to estimate the probability that, when encountering a given lemma, it is a part of a polar segment. Assuming we have that probability for each lemma we encounter in a given segment, we can by means of some aggregation, for instance a simple sum, easily decide whether to classify the given segment as polar. Then we can analogously determine its orientation. The desired properties of an indicative strength function are satisfied by lemma precision (see Wiebe et al., 2004). Then we need to compute a baseline for our lexicon, i.e. the probability that a randomly chosen word implicates the given polarity.

The classifier uses a standard unigram bag-of-words model, simply summing the indicator strength measurements over all the lemmas in a given segment. Then it selects the polarity class with the highest accumulated value in the desired measure. We have also employed a number of simple filters and other methods in order to improve the automatic annotation: filtering by frequency, weighed filtering by frequency (where the threshold for accepting a lemma as a feature is weighed by the baselines so that smaller polarity classes do not get discriminated), statistical significance filtering (where we accept a lemma if we can exclude the hypothesis that it is evenly distributed across polarity classes at a given level – 0.999, 0.95 and 0.8) or filtering by part of speech. Also, we have attempted to deal with sentence-level negation: first, if a segment contained a negative verb, the values for positive and negative polarity would be reversed for the segment, and a less crude method where we would specify which parts of speech to the right of a negative verb we would like to reverse.

5 Error Analysis

5.1 System Errors

Unfortunately, the first-aid filtering methods have proven rather useless – even those which appeared promising when we took a closer look into the list of incorrectly detected instances. For example, we found a number of functional words assigned with a wrong polarity. Nevertheless, when we removed them from the classification, the overall results did not improve. Moreover, when we started to eliminate the content words, the results got even worse. In order to reveal the main cause of the mistakes, we had to get back into the data once again.

We discovered various reasons of the system errors which can be divided into following categories. Statistically, the significant source of errors are still the short segments like *"Nothing"*, *"Price"* or *"I don't know"* which appear in both positive and negative reviews. These can by classified by the simple majority vote. If the vote is equal, the lemma classification is based on the baseline.

Also, some of these short segments have pretty high indicative strength for one polarity, but they often appear in the reviews expressing opposite evaluation (so filtering by frequency does not help):

<dg_postnegativetext>Proti:Kvalita.</dg_post negativetext>

<dg_postnegativetext>Cons:Quality.</dg_post negativetext>

In these cases the system always assigns the incorrect value. The solution to these problems could be elimination of all one-word answers or assigning the polarity of these items according to the polarity they have in subjectivity lexicon for Czech (see Veselovská, 2013).

One of the most frequented wrongly detected short phrases was *"High price"* tagged by the classifier with a positive instead of negative value. Besides, the classifier sometimes could not detect the domain-dependent evaluation, like *"long washing programs"*. These cases could be solved by using n-grams instead of just unigrams. Using n-grams could also hold for incorrectly detected evaluative idioms ("Je to sázka na jistotu" – *"It is a safe bet"* etc.) which are not listed in the Czech subjectivity lexicon or which are domain-dependent.

Furthermore, it could be advantageous to apply a coefficient for the initial and terminal position of words in a given segment. According to the reviews, it seems that the words occurring at the beginning or in the final parts of the text are more predictive towards the overall polarity:

<dg_postpositivetext>Pro: Je to výkonný a kvalitní vysavač, vím to, protože jsem ho měla víc jak deset let, ale bohužel se častým používáním porouchal a nechtěla jsem ho nechat opravovat, tak jsem si koupila nový. Ten starý vysavač funguje pořád jako vysavač, nejdou s ním čistit koberce. Půjčovala a půjčuje si ho celá rodina i příbuzný, je fakt dobrý, mohu ho doporučit.</dg_postpositivetext>

<dg_postpositivetext>Pros: It is a high-performance and quality vacuum cleaner, I am sure, because I had it for more than ten years, but unfortunately it got destroyed by the frequent use and I did not want to have it fixed, so I bought a new one. I still use the old one, but it is not possible to clean the carpets with it. The whole family borrows it constantly, it is really good and I can only recommend it. </dg_postpositivetext>

Moreover, the system is at the moment not able to treat emoticons: it considers every part of the smiley to be a separate word. To find positive and negative emoticons could help to detect given sentiment much better, as outlined in Read (2005).

There are also errors that can be improved using some simple linguistic features. We have already worked with sentential negation, using the rule roughly saying that all the negated verbs switch the overall polarity of the given sentence. But there are still plenty of rules which could be further implemented. Mostly, this concerns syntactic features. We found many incorrectly detected adversative constructions like:

<dg_postpositivetext>Pro: Není to žádný luxusní model, ale na chalupu stačí. </dg_postpositivetext>

<dg_postpositivetext>Pro: It is not a luxurious model, but for the cottage it will do. </dg_postpositivetext>

The "but" sentences can be as well solved by the rule, as indicated already in Hatzivassiloglou and McKeown (1997).

Also, there were many incorrectly evaluated concessive or conditional sentences in the data:

<dg_postpositivetext> Přestože neplní hlavní funkci kvůli které jsem ho kupoval (uklidit jednu místnost po druhé během naší nepřítomnosti), tak se jedná o jednoho z nejlepších robotů v nabídce na našem trhu. <dg_postpositivetext>

<dg_postpositivetext> Although it is not suitable for the function I bought it for (to clean the rooms one by one when we are not at home), it is still one of the best available robots. <dg_postpositivetext>

These problems might be eliminated by creating a stop-words list of items signalling non-evaluative part of the sentence.

5.2 Errors Caused by Human Annotators

Quite often, the reviewers were not evaluating given product, but they were rather commenting on something completely else:

<dg_postpositivetext>Pro: nemohu hodnotit, zboží jsem pro poškození vrátil </dg_postpositivetext>

<dg_postpositivetext>Pro:I cannot review this, I sent the goods back since it was damaged. </dg_postpositivetext>

or:

<dg_postpositivetext>Pro: Meteostanici mám jako dárek pro manžela, vyzkoušela jsem ji jen krátce při převzetí, tak se ještě nemůžu spolehlivě vyjádřit</dg_postpositivetext>

<dg_postpositivetext>Pro: I bought the meteostation as a present for my husband and I tried it out just quickly after I received it, so I cannot review it yet. </dg_postpositivetext>

On the other hand, we also noticed cases when the system classified the review correctly anyway:

<dg_postpositivetext>Pro: Přednosti tato pračka nemá.</dg_postpositivetext>

<dg_postpositivetext>Pro: This washing machine has no pluses. </dg_postpositivetext>

This kind of problems is tightly connected to pragmatics, but it might be partly solved by the reliable target detection.

The very common instances on which the classifier failed were the reviews in which people quoted other reviewers:

<dg_postpositivetext>Pro: Někdo píše SNAD dobrá značka???? Tato značka je mezi mraznicemi a ledniceni jednoznačná 1 </dg_postpositivetext>

<dg_postpositivetext>Pro: Anyone said QUITE good brand???? This brand is number one among freezers and fridges </dg_postpositivetext>

This is the matter of reliable finding of different sources of evaluation.

Some of the reviews contained besides other things the implicit evaluation:

<dg_postpositivetext>Pro: Nevím, jak jsem mohla bez sušičky být. Haní ji jen ten kdo ji nemá, nebo zhrzená manželka, když jí nechce manžel sušičku koupit. Úspora času, sice něco se musí žehlit, ale minimálně. Za sobotu jsem stihla usušit ložní prádlo, včetně obalů z matrací a lůžkovin (polštáře, deky) a ještě jsem měla spoustu času.</dg_postpositivetext>

<dg_postpositivetext>Pro:I don't know how I could have lived without the dryer. Only those who don't have it defame it, or the turned down wives whose husbands don't want to buy it for them. It saves time, some things still need to be ironed, but very little. I dried the bed linen during Saturday, including the mattress and bed linen cases (pillows, blankets) and I still had plenty of time. </dg_postpositivetext>

Unfortunately, the implicit evaluation is again connected to pragmatics and so far it seems to be one of the most difficult subtasks in sentiment analysis in general. However, the reviewers (at least on the Mall.cz retail server) did not tend to use it more often than prototypical explicit evaluation.

6 Conclusion and Future Work

We have analyzed different types of classifier errors on the real evaluative data and suggested various improvements. In the next step of the research, we would like to use n-grams to find the domain-dependent evaluative constructions and evaluative idioms. Also, we would like to detect the unmarked neutral segments by employing the simple heuristic model – e.g. when the system detects expressions like *"I don't know"*. If the segment has less than five words, it will be classified as neutral.

In addition, we realized that it is necessary to implement the detection of emoticons and treat particular parts of adversative constructions separately. Moreover, it seems unavoidable to apply the model for the reliable detection of targets and sources of evaluation, e.g. by employing methods for detecting thematic concentration of the text (see Čech et al., 2013).

References

Choi, Yejin & Claire Cardie (2008). *Learning with compositional semantics as structural inference for subsentential sentiment analysis.* In Proceedings of the Conference on Empirical Methods in Natural Language Processing (pp 793-801).

Cui, Hang, Mittal, Vibhu, & Datar, Mayur (2006). *Comparative experiments on sentiment classification for online product reviews.* In AAAI (Vol. 6, pp. 1265-1270).

Čech, Radek, Popescu, Ioan-Iovitz & Gabriel Altmann (2013). *Methods of analysis of a thematic concentration of the text.* Czech and Slovak Linguistic Review. (in press).

Habernal, Ivan, Ptáček, Tomáš & Josef Steinberger (2013). *Sentiment Analysis in Czech Social Media Using Supervised Machine Learning.* In Proceedings of the 4th Workshop on Computational Approaches to Subjectivity, Sentiment and Social Media Analysis (pp 65-74).

Hajič, Jan (2004). *Disambiguation of rich inflection: computational morphology of Czech.* Karolinum.

Hatzivassiloglou, Vasileios & Kathleen McKeown, (1997). *Predicting the semantic orientation of adjectives.* In Proceedings of the 35th Annual Meeting of the Association for Computational Linguistics and Eighth Conference of the European Chapter of the Association for Computational Linguistics (pp. 174-181). Association for Computational Linguistics.

Johansson, Richard & Alessandro Moschitti (2013). *Relational features in fine-grained opinion analysis.* Computational Linguistics 39 (3).

Liu, Bing (2010). *Sentiment Analysis and Subjectivity.* Invited Chapter for the Handbook of Natural Language Processing, Second Edition. Marcel Dekker, Inc: New York.

Moilanen, Karo & Stephen Pulman (2007). *Sentiment composition.* In Proceedings of the Recent Advances in Natural Language Processing International Conference (pp 378-382).

Polanyi, Livia & Annie Zaenen (2004). *Contextual valence shifters.* In Working Notes of the AAAI Spring Symposium on Exploring Attitude and Affect in Text: Theories and Applications.

Read, Jonathon (2005). *Using emoticons to reduce dependency in machine learning techniques for sentiment classification.* In Proceedings of the ACL Student Research Workshop (pp. 43-48). Association for Computational Linguistics.

Veselovská, Kateřina (2012). *Sentence-level sentiment analysis in Czech.* In Proceedings of the 2nd International Conference on Web Intelligence, Mining and Semantics.

Veselovská, Kateřina, Hajič, Jan Jr. & Jana Šindlerová (2012). *Creating annotated resources for polarity classification in Czech.* In Proceedings of KONVENS (pp. 296-304).

Veselovská, Kateřina (2013). *Czech Subjectivity Lexicon: A Lexical Resource for Czech Polarity Classification.* In Proceedings of SLOVKO 2013.

Wiebe, Janyce, Wilson, Theresa, Bruce, Rebecca, Bell, Matthew, & Martin, Melanie (2004). *Learning subjective language.* Computational linguistics, 30 (3) (pp. 277-308).

Topic Modeling with Sentiment Clues and Relaxed Labeling Schema

Yasuhide Miura
Fuji Xerox Co., Ltd., Japan
yasuhide.miura
@fujixerox.co.jp

Keigo Hattori
Fuji Xerox Co., Ltd., Japan
keigo.hattori
@fujixerox.co.jp

Tomoko Ohkuma
Fuji Xerox Co., Ltd., Japan
ohkuma.tomoko
@fujixerox.co.jp

Hiroshi Masuichi
Fuji Xerox Co., Ltd., Japan
hiroshi.masuichi
@fujixerox.co.jp

Abstract

This paper proposes a method to extract sentiment topics from a text collection. The method utilizes *sentiment clues* and a *relaxed labeling schema* to extract sentiment topics. Experiments with a quantitative and a qualitative evaluations was done to confirm the performance of the method. The quantitative evaluation with a polarity classification marked the accuracy of 0.701 in tweets and 0.691 in newswire texts. These performances are comparable to support vector machine baselines. The qualitative evaluation of polarity topic extraction showed an overall accuracy of 0.729, and a higher accuracy of 0.889 for positive topic extraction. The result indicates the efficacy of our method in extracting sentiment topics.

1 Introduction

Continuous increase of text data arose an interest to develop a method to automatically analyze a large collection of texts. Topic modeling methods such as Latent Dirichlet Allocation (LDA)(Blei et al., 2003) are popular methods for such analysis. For example, they have been applied to analyze newswire topics (Blei et al., 2003; Rajagopal et al., 2013), scientific topics (Griffiths and Steyvers, 2004), weblogs (Mei et al., 2007), online reviews (Titov and McDonald, 2008b), and microblogs (Ramage et al., 2010; Zhao et al., 2011). Topic modeling methods generally extract probability distributions of word as *topics* of a given text collection. Note that this definition is quite different from the definitions in sentiment analysis or opinion mining literatures (Yi et al., 2003; Kim and Hovy, 2006; Stoyanov and Cardie, 2008; Das and Bandyopadhyay, 2010a; Das and Bandyopadhyay, 2010b) which basically define *topic* as an object of an opinion. Extracted topics are useful as a summary to catch a broad image of a text collection, but they are not always intuitively interpretable by humans. Typical methods for estimating topic modeling parameters aim to maximize a likelihood of training data (Blei et al., 2003; Griffiths and Steyvers, 2004). This objective is known to form topics that are not always most semantically meaningful (Chang et al., 2009).

Approaches to extract more explicit topics using observed labels are being proposed. Supervised LDA (Blei and McAuliffe, 2007), Labeled LDA (Ramage et al., 2009), and Partially Labeled Dirichlet Allocation (PLDA)(Ramage et al., 2011) are such supervised topic models. Labels of these supervised topic models are not required to be *strictly* designed. Strictly designed labels here mean organized and controlled labels like the categories of Reuters Corpora (Lewis et al., 2004). Ramage et al. (2009) and Ramage et al. (2010) showed the effectiveness of using labels like del.icio.us tags, Twitter hashtags, and emoticons. The use of these non-strict labels can avoid cost-intensive manual annotations of labels. However, available labels completely depend on a community that provides them. This is problematic when a text collection to analyze is already specified since we may not find labels that are suitable for an analysis.

Sentiment labels such as a product rating and a service rating are widely used labels that are community dependent. For example, a hotel may be positively rated for food but be negatively rated for room. These labels have been used successfully to extract sentiments of various aspects (Blei and McAuliffe, 2007; Titov and McDonald, 2008a). However, these kind of rating labels can not be expected to exist in communities other than review

Proceedings of the 3rd Workshop on Sentiment Analysis where AI meets Psychology (SAAIP 2013), IJCNLP 2013, pages 6–14,
Nagoya, Japan, October 14, 2013.

sites.

This paper presents a method to extract sentiment topics from a text collection. A noticeable characteristic of our method is that it does not require strictly designed sentiment labels. The method uses *sentiment clues* and a *relaxed labeling schema* to extract sentiment topics. Sentiment clue here denotes meta data or a lexical characteristic that strongly relates to a certain sentiment. Some examples of sentiment clues are: a happy face emoticon that usually expresses a positive sentiment and a social tag[1] of a disaster that tends to bear negative sentiment. Sentiment label here is expected to be label that expresses a general sentiment like positive, neutral, or negative. Relaxed labeling schema is a schema that defines a process of setting labels to a text using the given sentiment clues. The key feature of this schema is that a text with a sentiment clue gets a sentiment-clue-specific label and a sentiment label. This assumes that words that co-occur with a sentiment clue tend to hold the same sentiment as the sentiment clue. The assumption follows an idea from supervised sentiment classification methods of Go et al. (2009), Read (2005), and Davidov et al. (2010) which presume strong relationships between certain emoticons and certain sentiments.

Our contributions in this paper are two-fold: (1) we propose a method that does not require strictly designed sentiment labels to extract sentiment topics from a text collection, (2) we show the effectiveness of our method by performing experiments with a quantitative and a qualitative evaluations. The rest of this paper is organized as follows. Section 2 describes our method in detail. Section 3 explains data that are used in the experiment of the method. Section 4 demonstrates the effectiveness of the method with an experiment. Section 5 indicates related works of the method. Section 6 concludes the paper with some future extensions to the method.

2 Methods

2.1 Partially Labeled Dirichlet Allocation

Our method utilizes PLDA (Ramage et al., 2011) as a supervised topic modeling method. PLDA is an extension of LDA (Blei et al., 2003) which is an unsupervised machine learning method that models topics of a document collection. LDA assumes that documents can be expressed as an mixture of topics, where a topic is a distribution over words. PLDA incorporates supervision to LDA by constraining the use of topic with observed labels. The generative process of PLDA shown in Figure 1 is as follows:

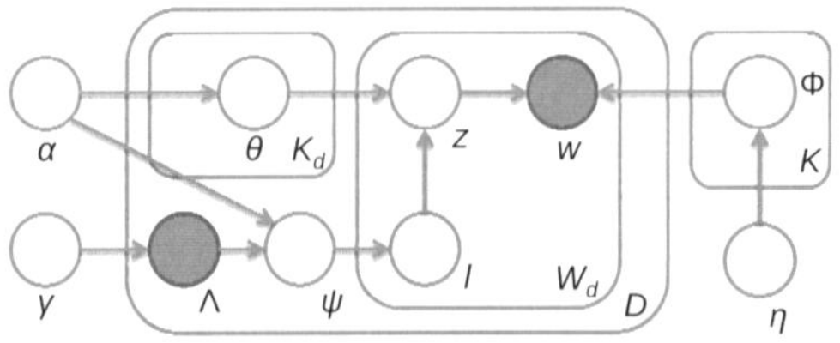

Figure 1: The graphical model of PLDA. Shaded elements represent observed elements.

For each topic $k \in \{1 \dots K\}$
  Pick $\Phi_k \sim \mathrm{Dir}(\eta)$
For each document $d \in \{1 \dots D\}$
  For each document label $j \in \Lambda_d$ (observed labels)
    Pick $\theta_{d,j} \sim \mathrm{Dir}(\alpha)$
  Pick $|\Lambda_d|$ size $\psi_d \sim \mathrm{Dir}(\alpha)$
  For each word $w \in W_d$
    Pick label $l \sim \mathrm{Mult}(\psi_d)$
    Pick topic $z \sim \mathrm{Mult}(\theta_{d,l})$
    Pick word $w \sim \mathrm{Mult}(\Phi_z)$

In the process, $\mathrm{Dir}(\cdot)$ represents a Dirichlet distribution and $\mathrm{Mult}(\cdot)$ represents a multinomial distribution.

The learning process of PLDA will be a problem to estimate parameters Φ, ψ, θ that maximizes the joint likelihood $P(\mathbf{w}, \mathbf{z}, \mathbf{l}|\mathbf{\Lambda}, \alpha, \eta, \gamma)$ of a given document collection. An efficient method for estimating these parameters are presented in Ramage et al. (2011).

2.2 Proposed Method

We propose a simple three step method to extract sentiment topics from a text collection.

Step 1: Preparation of Sentiment Clues

Firstly, a set of sentiment clue is prepared. Typical examples of sentiment clues are emoticons and social tags. Table 1 shows an example of a sentiment clue set.

Step 2: Relaxed Labeling Schema

Secondly, labels are set to texts using the sentiment clue set defined in Step 1. Labels are set

[1]Social tag here means a non-strict tag that is defined in a web community (e.g. a del.icio.us tag or a Twitter hashtag).

Sentiment Clue	Clue Name	Sentiment Label
:-)	happy face emoticon	positive
:-(	sad face emoticon	negative

Table 1: An example of a sentiment clue set.

to text differently in condition of sentiment clue existence. A text with a sentiment clue gets a sentiment-clue-specific label and a sentiment label that corresponds to it. For example, with the sentiment clue set of Table 1, a text including :-) gets a *happy face emoticon* label and a *positive* label. A text without any sentiment clue gets all sentiment labels that are defined in Step 1. For example, with the sentiment clue set of Table 1, a text that does not include :-) and :-(gets a *positive* and a *negative* labels. Table 2 summarizes how labels are set to texts. The basic policy of this process is to label texts with all possible labels. We call this schema *relaxed labeling schema* because this all-possible policy is non-strict, thus *relaxed*.

Step 3: Supervised Topic Modeling

Thirdly, a supervised topic modeling using PLDA is processed to the labeled texts of Step 2. Sentiment topics will be extracted as the topics that are labeled by the sentiment labels of Step 1. Note that our method is not fully dependent to PLDA. An alternate supervised topic modeling method that allows multiple labels to a text can be used instead of PLDA.

3 Data

We performed an experiment to confirm the effectiveness of the proposed method. Prior to explaining the details of the experiment, we will describe data that we used in it.

3.1 Emoticon Polarity List

We have done a preliminary investigation of emoticons to define sentiment clues. Firstly, we picked up six emoticons that are widely used in Japanese. Secondly, 300 tweets, 50 per emoticon, that include one of the six emoticons were annotated by three annotators with one of the following four polarities: positive, negative, positive and negative, and neutral. Thirdly, the number of positive annotations and negative annotations that two annotators or more agreed were counted for each emoticons. Table 3 shows polarity annotations that

Emoticon	Polarity
(´ ▽ `)ノ	positive
＼(^o^)／	positive
(^-^)	positive
orz	negative
(´ · ω · `)	negative
(>_<)	negative

Table 3: The six emoticons and their largest vote polarities.

Criterion	Tweets
HAPPY	10,000
SAD	10,000
NO-EMO	200,000
total	220,000

Table 4: The summary of the topic modeling data.

each of the emoticons got the largest vote.

3.2 Topic Modeling Data

Tweets are used as the topic modeling data of the proposed method. *Public streams* tweets in Japanese during the period of May 2011– August 2011 are collected using the Twitter streaming API [2]. From there, we sampled total of 220,000 tweets that satisfy one of the following three criteria:

HAPPY 10,000 tweets that contain (´ ▽ `)ノ (a happy emoticon in Japanese, here on EMO-HAPPY).

SAD 10,000 tweets that contain orz (a sad emoticon in Japanese, here on EMO-SAD).

NO-EMO 200,000 tweets that do not contain any emoticon[3]. For this criterion, following two conditions were also considered: a tweet consists of five words or more and a tweet is not a retweet. These conditions are set to reduce the number of uninformative tweets and duplicate tweets.

In the sampling of NO-EMO, a Japanese morphology analyzer Kuromoji[4] is used for word segmentation. Table 4 shows the summary of the sampled tweets.

[2]https://dev.twitter.com/docs/streaming-apis

[3]10,924 Japanese emoticons which we collected from several web sites are used in this process.

[4]http://www.atilika.org/

Text Type	HFE label	positive label	negative label	SFE label
Texts with the happy face emoticon	√	√		
Texts without any emoticon		√	√	
Texts with the sad face emoticon			√	√

Table 2: The summary of how labels are set to texts with the sentiment clues of Table 1. In the table HFE is "happy face emoticon" and SFE is "sad face emoticon".

3.3 Polarity Classification Evaluation Data

Two data sets, *Tweet* and *Newswire*, are used to evaluate the performance of polarity classification. Tweet is an evaluation set of general tweets whose domain is same as the topic modeling data. Newswire is an evaluation set of newswire texts whose domain is quite different from the topic modeling data. The details of these sets are described in the following subsections.

3.3.1 Tweet

3,000 tweets satisfying the following three conditions are sampled from the May 2011–August 2011 tweets of Section 3.2:

a. A tweet consists of five words or more (same as NO-EMO).

b. A tweet includes an adjective, an adverb, an adnominal, or a noun-adverbial. This condition expects to increase the number of tweets that include evaluative content.

c. A tweet does not have a POS tag that composes more than 80% of its words. This condition is set to exclude tweets such as a list of nouns or an interjection that includes a repeated character.

Note that words and their POS tags are extracted using Kuromoji like in NO-EMO.

The sampled 3,000 tweets were annotated with one of the following six polarity labels: positive, negative, positive and negative, neutral, advertisement, and uninterpretable. Label *advertisement* is defined to avoid annotating an advertising tweet to positive. Label *uninterpretable* is defined to prevent annotating a tweet that requires its accompanying context to determine a polarity.

Eighteen annotators formed ten pairs[5] and each pair annotated 300 tweets. The annotation agreement was 0.417 in Cohen's Kappa. We extracted 723 tweets that two annotators agreed with positive or negative as polarity classification evaluation data. Tweet in table 5 shows the composition of the data.

[5]Two annotators participated in two pairs.

Type	Polarity	Number
Tweet	Positive	384
	Negative	339
Newswire	Positive	107
	Negative	327

Table 5: The compositions of the polarity classification evaluation data.

3.3.2 Newswire

434 sentences of the Japanese section of NTCIR-7 Multilingual Opinion Analysis Task (MOAT) (Seki et al., 2008) that satisfies the following condition is extracted:

a. A sentence with a positive or a negative polarity that two or more annotators agreed.

The Japanese section consists of 7,163 sentences from Mainichi Newspaper. Polarities are annotated to these sentences by three annotators. Note that the sentences are newswire texts, and are mostly non-subjective or neutral polarity. Newswire in table 5 shows the composition of the data.

4 Experiment

We performed an experiment and two evaluations to confirm the effectiveness of the proposed method.

4.1 Sentiment Clues

The sentiment clue set of Table 6 was used in the experiment. Note that the topic modeling data include 10,000 tweets that contain EMO-HAPPY and 10,000 tweets that contain EMO-SAD since they are used in the sampling process of them (Section 3.2).

Sentiment Clue	Sentiment Label
EMO-HAPPY	positive
EMO-SAD	negative

Table 6: The sentiment clues used in the experiment.

4.2 Preprocesses

Number of preprocesses were done to the topic modeling data to extract words from them.

1. Following normalizations are applied to the texts: Unicode normalization in form NFKC[6], repeated 'w's (a character used to express laugh in casual Japanese) are replaced with 'ww', a Twitter user name (e.g. @user) is replaced with 'USER', a hashtag (e.g. #hashtag) is replaced with 'HASHTAG', and a URL (e.g. http://example.org) is replaced with 'URL'.
2. Words and their POS tags are extracted from the texts using Kuromoji.
3. Words that do not belong to the following POS tags are removed (stop POS tag process): noun[7], verb, adjective, adverb, adnominal, interjection, filler, symbol-alphabet, and unknown.
4. Six very common stop words such as *suru* "do" and *naru* "become" are removed.
5. The words are replaced with their base forms to reduce conjugational variations.
6. Words that appeared twice or less in the data are removed.

4.3 Supervised Topic Modeling

Stanford Topic Modeling Toolbox[8] is used as an implementation of PLDA. For the priors of PLDA, symmetric topic prior α and symmetric word prior η were set to 0.01. Number of topics for each labels were set to the numbers listed in Table 7. *Background* in the table is a special topic that can be used to generate words in any documents (tweets) regardless of their sentiment labels. In supervised topic modeling, this kind of topic can be used to extract label independent topic (Ramage et al., 2010).

[6]http://unicode.org/reports/tr15/

[7]There are some exceptions like name suffixes that are nouns but are removed.

[8]http://www-nlp.stanford.edu/software/tmt/tmt-0.4/

Label	Number
positive	50
negative	50
EMO-HAPPY	1
EMO-SAD	1
background	1

Table 7: The number of topics set to each labels.

The parameter estimation of PLDA is done to the preprocessed data using CVB0 variation approximation (Asuncion et al., 2009) with max iteration set to 1000. Table 8 shows some examples of the extracted topics.

4.4 Evaluations

4.4.1 Quantitative Evaluation of Topics

A discriminative polarity classification was performed as a quantitative evaluation. Note that this evaluation dose not directly evaluate the performance of a sentiment topic extraction. However, following the previous works that jointly modeled sentiment and topic (Lin et al., 2012; Jo and Oh, 2011), we perform a sentiment classification evaluation. A more direct evaluation will be presented in Section 4.4.2.

Using the parameter estimated topic model, document-topic distribution inferences were conducted to the polarity classification evaluation data described in Section 3.3. From there, a positive and a negative score were calculated for each tweet with the following equation:

$$score(d, l) = \sum_{t_l} P(t_l|d) \quad (1)$$

In the equation, d is a document (tweet), l is a label (either positive or negative), t_l is a topic of l, and $P(t_l|d)$ is the posterior probability of t_l given d. For each tweet, a label that maximizes Equation 1 was set as a classification label.

We also prepared a baseline support vector machine (SVM) based polarity detector similar to Go et al. (2009) for a comparison. HAPPY criterion tweets and SAD criterion tweets of Section 3.2 are used as the positive samples and the negative samples of SVM respectively. Following the best accuracy setting of Go et al. (2009), only bag-of-word unigrams were used as the features of SVM. For preprocesses, same preprocesses as the proposed method (Section 4.2) with EMO-HAPPY and EMO-SAD emoticons added to the

Label	Probable Words (Top 10)
EMO-HAPPY	(´ ▽ `) ノ [EMO-HAPPY], USER [normalized user name], ない "no", ん [interjection], ?, の "thing", w [laugh expression], ww [laugh expression], 笑 "laugh", ... [ellipsis]
EMO-SAD	orz [EMO-SAD], USER [normalized user name], !, ー [macron], (,), ... [ellipsis], ° [degree symbol], Д [a character often used in Japanese emoticons], 行く "go"
positive #11	USER [normalized user name], 食べる "eat", 美味しい "delicious", 飲む "drink", 屋 "shop", 料理 "meal", ラーメン "ramen", 店 "shop", コーヒー "coffee", 肉 "meat"
positive #30	!, USER [normalized user name], ありがとう "thank you", よろしく "please", お願い "please", くださる [honorific word], イイ "good", これから "from now", 楽しむ "enjoy", できる "can"
negative #2	さ [suffix similar to -ness], 暑い "hot", 夏 "summer", この "this", そう [reply word], 中 "inside", 今日 "today", 風 "wind", 外 "outside", 汗 "sweat"
negative #48	くる "happen", 目 "eye", 痛い "hurt", 入る "enter", 風呂 "bath", 寝る "sleep", 頭 "head", お腹 "stomach", すぎる "too", ない "no"

Table 8: Examples of extracted labeled topics with Table 7 setting. Bracketed expressions in the table are English explanations of preceding Japanese words that can not be directly translated.

Type	Method	Accuracy
Tweet	Majority Baseline	0.531
	Proposed	0.701
	SVM	0.705
Newswire	Majority Baseline	0.753
	Proposed	0.691
	SVM	0.712

Table 9: The polarity classification results. The majority baseline is the case when all predictions were same. This is positive for Tweet and negative for Newswire.

stop words. These two emoticons are added to stop words since they are used as the labels of this SVM baseline. As an implementation of SVM, LIBLINEAR[9] was used with L2-loss linear SVM and the cost parameter C set to 1.0.

Table 9 shows the results of polarity classifications. The proposed method marked an accuracy of 0.701 in Tweet, which is comparable to 0.705 of the SVM baseline. An accuracy was 0.691 for Newswire which is also comparable to 0.712 of the SVM baseline. However, the simple majority baseline has the highest accuracy of 0.753 in Newswire.

4.4.2 Qualitative Evaluation of Topics

The quantitative evaluation evaluated the performance of the sentiment topic extraction indirectly with the sentiment classification. As a more direct qualitative evaluation, two persons manually evaluated the extracted 50 positive and 50 negative topics.

The evaluators were presented with *top 40 probable words* and *top 20 probable tweets* for each topic. Top 40 probable words of topic t_l were simply the top 40 words of the topic-word distribution $P(w|t_l)$. The extraction of top 20 probable tweets were more complex compared to the extraction of words. Document-topic distribution inferences were run to the training data using the parameter estimated topic model. For each topic t_l, top 20 tweets of document-topic distribution $P(t_l|d)$ were extracted as the top 20 probable tweets of t_l.

The evaluators labeled positive, negative, or uninterpretable to each of the topics by examining the presented information. The evaluators are instructed to label positive, negative, or uninterpretable. Label *uninterpretable* is an exceptional label. Topics with probable words and tweets that satisfy one of the following conditions were labeled uninterpretable: (a) majority of them are not in Japanese (b) majority of them are interjections or onomatopoeias, and (c) majority of them are neutral.

The agreement of the two evaluations was 0.406 in Cohen's Kappa. We extracted 59 topics that the two evaluators agreed with positive or negative, and measured the accuracies of the 50 positive and 50 negative topics. Table 10 shows the detail of the evaluation result. The overall accuracy was 0.729,

[9] http://www.csie.ntu.edu.tw/~cjlin/liblinear/

Label	#P	#N	Accuracy
positive	24	3	0.889
negative	13	19	0.594
overall			0.729

Table 10: The evaluation result of the 50 positive topics and the 50 negative topics. #P and #N are the number of topics that the two evaluators agreed as positive and negative respectively.

which indicates the success of the sentiment topics extraction.

5 Related Works

There are several works that simultaneously modeled topic and sentiment. Mei et al. (2007) proposed Topic Sentiment Mixture (TSM) model which is a multinomial mixture model that mixes topic models and a sentiment model. Lin et al. (2012) proposed joint sentiment-topic model (JSTM) that extends LDA to jointly model topic and sentiment. Jo and Oh (2011) proposed Aspect and Sentiment Unification Model (ASUM) that adapts LDA to model aspect and sentiment pairs. Titov and McDonald (2008a) proposed Multi-Aspect Sentiment (MAS) model that models topic with observed aspect ratings and latent overall sentiment ratings. Blei and McAuliffe (2007) proposed supervised LDA (sLDA) that can handle sentiments as observed labels. Our method is different from TSM model, JSTM, and ASUM since these models handle sentiments as latent variables. MAS model and sLDA utilize sentiments explicitly like in our method. However, not like in the relaxed labeling schema of our method, they have not presented a technique specialized for non-strict labels.

Sentiment analysis (Pang and Lee, 2008) also has a close relationship with our method. We borrowed the idea of using sentiment clues from sentiment analysis methods of Go et al. (2009), Read (2005), and Davidov et al. (2010). Our method is different from these method in the objective that the method aims to extract sentiment topics, not sentiments, from a text collection.

6 Conclusion

We proposed a method to extract sentiment topics using sentiment clues and the relaxed labeling schema. The quantitative evaluation with the polarity classification marked the accuracy of 0.701 in tweets and the accuracy of 0.691 in newswire texts. These performances are comparable to the SVM baselines 0.705 and 0.712 respectively. The qualitative evaluation of sentiment topics showed the overall accuracy of 0.729. The result indicates the success in the extraction of sentiment topics. However, compared to the high accuracy of 0.889 achieved in the extraction of positive topics, the extraction of negative topics showed the moderate accuracy of 0.594.

One characteristic of our method is that the method only requires a small set of sentiment clues to extract sentiment topics. Even though the method has its basis on a supervised topic modeling method, cost-intensive manual annotations of labels are not necessary. Despite the weakness of extracting negative topics shown in the qualitative evaluation, we think this highly applicable nature makes our method a convenient method. For future extensions of the method, we are planning the following two works:

Extraction of Aspect Topics

In this paper, we proposed a method that extracts sentiment topics using sentiment clues. Similar approach can be taken to extract non-sentiment topics if there are *clues* for them. For example, Twitter communities use hashtags to group variety of topics (Ramage et al., 2010). As a future work, we are planning to perform an aspect topic extraction using social tags as aspect clues.

Introduction of Non-parametric Bayesian Methods

In the experiment of our method, we set the equal number of topics to a positive and a negative labels. How polarities distribute should differ among domains, and this equal number setting may not work well on some domains. We are planning to introduce a non-parametric Bayesian method (Blei and Jordan, 2005; Ramage et al., 2011) to our method so that the number of topics can be decided automatically.

References

Arthur Asuncion, Max Welling, Padhraic Smyth, and Yee Whye Teh. 2009. On smoothing and inference for topic models. In *Proceedings of the Twenty-Fifth Conference on Uncertainty in Artificial Intelligence*, pages 27–34.

David M. Blei and Michael I. Jordan. 2005. Variational inference for Dirichlet process mixtures. *Bayesian Analysis*, 1:121–144.

David M. Blei and Jon D. McAuliffe. 2007. Supervised topic models. In *Neural Information Processing Systems 20*, pages 121–128.

David M. Blei, Andrew Y. Ng, and Michael I. Jordan. 2003. Latent Dirichlet allocation. *Journal of Machine Learning Research*, 3:993–1022.

Jonathan Chang, Jordan Boyd-Graber, Sean Gerrish, Chong Wang, and David M. Blei. 2009. Reading tea leaves: how humans interpret topic models. In *Neural Information Processing Systems 22*, pages 288–296.

Dipankar Das and Sivaji Bandyopadhyay. 2010a. Extracting emotion topics from blog sentences: use of voting from multi-engine supervised classifiers. In *Proceedings of the 2nd international workshop on Search and mining user-generated contents*, pages 119–126.

Dipankar Das and Sivaji Bandyopadhyay. 2010b. Identifying emotion topic - an unsupervised hybrid approach with rhetorical structure and heuristic classifier. In *Proceedings of The 6th International Conference on Natural Language Processing and Knowledge Engineering*.

Dmitry Davidov, Oren Tsur, and Ari Rappoport. 2010. Enhanced sentiment learning using twitter hashtags and smileys. In *Proceedings of the 23rd International Conference on Computational Linguistics: Posters*, pages 241–249.

Alec Go, Richa Bhayani, and Lei Huang. 2009. Twitter sentiment classification using distant supervision. Technical report, Stanford University.

Thomas L. Griffiths and Mark Steyvers. 2004. Finding scientific topics. *Proceedings of the National Academy of Sciences*, 101(Suppl 1):5228–5235.

Yohan Jo and Alice Oh. 2011. Aspect and sentiment unification model for online review analysis. In *Proceedings of the fourth ACM international conference on Web search and data mining*, pages 815–824.

Soo-Min Kim and Eduard Hovy. 2006. Extracting opinions, opinion holders, and topics expressed in online news media text. In *Proceedings of the Workshop on Sentiment and Subjectivity in Text*, pages 1–8.

David D. Lewis, Yiming Yang, Tony G. Rose, and Fan Li. 2004. RCV1: A new benchmark collection for text categorization research. *Journal of Machine Learning Research*, 5:361–397.

Chenghua Lin, Yulan He, Richard Everson, and Stefan Rùger. 2012. Weakly supervised joint sentiment-topic detection from text. *IEEE Transactions on Knowledge and Data Engineering*, 24(Issue 6):1134–1145.

Qiaozhu Mei, Xu Ling, Matthew Wondra, Hang Su, and ChengXiang Zhai. 2007. Topic sentiment mixture: modeling facets and opinions in weblogs. In *Proceedings of the 16th international conference on World Wide Web*, pages 171–180.

Bo Pang and Lillian Lee. 2008. Opinion mining and sentiment analysis. *Foundations and Trends in Information Retrieval*, 2(1-2):1–135.

Dheeraj Rajagopal, Daniel Olsher, Erik Cambria, and Kenneth Kwok. 2013. Commonsense-based topic modeling. In *Proceedings of the Second International Workshop on Issues of Sentiment Discovery and Opinion Mining*, pages 6:1–6:8.

Daniel Ramage, David Hall, Rameshi Nallapati, and Christopher D. Manning. 2009. Labeled LDA: A supervised topic model for credit attribution in multi-labeled corpora. In *Proceedings of the 2009 Conference on Empirical Methods in Natural Language Processing*, pages 248–256.

Daniel Ramage, Susan Dumais, and Dan Liebling. 2010. Characterizing microblogs with topic models. In *Proceedings of the fourth international AAAI conference on Weblogs and Social Media*, pages 130–137.

Daniel Ramage, Chistopher D. Manning, and Susan Dumais. 2011. Partially labeled topic models for interpretable text mining. In *Proceedings of the 17th ACM SIGKDD international conference on Knowledge discovery and data mining*, pages 457–465.

Jonathon Read. 2005. Using emoticons to reduce dependency in machine learning techniques for sentiment classification. In *Proceedings of the ACL Student Research Workshop*, pages 43–48.

Yohei Seki, David Kirk Evans, Lun-Wei Ku, Le Sun, Hsin-Hsi Chen, and Noriko Kando. 2008. Overview of multilingual opinion analysis task at NTCIR-7. In *Proceedings of the 7th NTCIR Workshop Meeting on Evaluation of Information Access Technologies: Information Retrieval, Question Answering, and Cross-Lingual Information Access*, pages 185–203.

Veselin Stoyanov and Claire Cardie. 2008. Annotating topics of opinions. In *Proceedings of the Sixth International Conference on Language Resources and Evaluation*, pages 3213–3217.

Ivan Titov and Ryan McDonald. 2008a. A joint model of text and aspect ratings for sentiment summarization. In *Proceedings of the 46th Annual Meeting of the Association for Computational Linguistics: Human Language Technologies*, pages 308–316.

Ivan Titov and Ryan McDonald. 2008b. Modeling online reviews with multi-grain topic models. In *Proceedings of the 17th international conference on World Wide Web*, pages 111–120.

Jeonghee Yi, Tetsuya Nasukawa, Razvan Bunescu, and Wayne Niblack. 2003. Sentiment analyzer: Extracting sentiments about a given topic using natural language processing techniques. In *Proceedings of the Third IEEE International Conference on Data Mining*, pages 427–434.

Wayne Xin Zhao, Jing Jiang, Jianshu Weng, Jing He, Ee-Peng Lim, Hongfei Yan, and Xiaoming Li. 2011. Comparing Twitter and traditional media using topic models. In *Proceedings of the 33rd European conference on Advances in information retrieval*, pages 338–349.

Bilingual analysis of LOVE and HATRED emotional markers (SPSS-based approach)

Nataliya Panasenko
Faculty of Mass Media Communication, University of SS Cyril and Methodius (UCM) in Trnava, Nám. J. Herdu, 2
Trnava Slovakia
cindy777@mail.ru

Andrej Trnka
Faculty of Mass Media Communication, UCM, Trnava, Nám. J. Herdu, 2
Trnava Slovakia
andrej.trnka@ucm.sk

Dana Petranová
Faculty of Mass Media Communication, UCM, Trnava, Nám. J. Herdu, 2
Trnava Slovakia
dana.petranova@gmail.com

Slavomír Magál
Faculty of Mass Media Communication, UCM, Trnava, Nám. J. Herdu, 2
Trnava Slovakia
slavomir.magal@ucm.sk

Abstract

This paper presents the results of GRID project which aimed at studying the semantics of 24 emotion terms in 23 languages belonging to 8 language families (Indo-European, Indo-Iranian, Afro-Asiatic, Altaic, Uralic, Japonic, Sino-Tibetan, Niger-Congo, and Unclassified). We limit ourselves in this article only to two Slavic languages – Slovak and Czech and to two emotion terms – love and hatred – and try show how greatly information technologies helped the psychologists first of all to obtain, and then to process large volume of information from a bit less than 5000 people, active project participants, who live in 30 countries.

1 Credits

Though two languages are discussed in the paper, it is written by teachers of Faculty of Mass Media Communication, University of SS Cyril and Methodius in Trnava, Slovakia: by prof. Nataliya Panasenko, assoc. prof. Slavomír Magál, Dr. Dana Petranová and Dr. Andrej Trnka.

2 Introduction

Feelings and emotions are important components of human cognitive activity, behaviour, communication with the world and other people. Human emotional sphere has been thoroughly analyzed by psychologists, philosophers, and linguists.

Outstanding scholars from different countries (Cornelius, 1996; Ellsworth and Nesse, 2009; Fontaine, Scherer et al. 2007; Frijda, 1986; Лук, 1972 and many others) have made a considerable contribution to creation theoretical and methodological basics of feelings and emotions study. Scholars have described the essence of emotions (Nakonečný, 2000; Scherer, 2005; Stuchlíková, 2007), have made their classification (Ahem and Schwarz, 1979; Додонов, 1975), have described some of them in details (Panasenko, 2012; Сарбаш, 2008), have studied them from cognitive (Byessonova, 2009; Ortoni, Clore and Collins, 1988) and cultural aspect (Fontaine, 2008; Kitayama, Markus et al., 1995; Ogarkova, Panasenko et al., 2013; Panasenko, Démuthová et al., 2012; Russel, 1991), specified their attitudinal character (Ewert, 1970), role and function of emotions in social life (Slaměník, 2005), means of their expression and perception (Рожкова, 1974), peculiarities of emotional sphere of people belonging to different professions (teachers, musicians, actors, doctors, TV announcers (Ильин, 2001).

In this article we want to show, what ways of emotion investigation have been recently employed by psychologists and what features describing emotions are important most of all for Slovaks and Czechs. Psychologists take into account different features accompanying emotions, such as *features describing the person's evalua-*

Proceedings of the 3rd Workshop on Sentiment Analysis where AI meets Psychology (SAAIP 2013), IJCNLP 2013, pages 15–23,
Nagoya, Japan, October 14, 2013.

tion or appraisal of the event, *features describing the bodily symptoms* that tend to occur during the emotional state (felt shivers in the neck or chest, got pale, felt his/her heartbeat slowing down, felt his/her heartbeat getting faster, felt his/her breathing getting faster, perspired, or had moist hands); *features describing facial and vocal expressions*, that accompany the emotion (blushed, smiled, felt his/her jaw drop, pressed his/her lips together, felt his/her eyebrows go up, frowned, closed his/her eyes, had tears in his/her eyes; changes in the loudness of voice, of speech melody, speech tempo, speech disturbances, etc.). All these symptoms are included into GRID project, results of which we present in our paper.

3 GRID project

The International GRID Research Consortium was founded in 2005 to organize a world-wide study of the semantics of emotion terms in different languages (French, Italian, Portuguese, Romansh, Spanish; Afrikaans, Dutch, English, German; Bulgarian, Czech, Polish, Russian, Slovak, Ukrainian; Greek; Hindi; Arabic, Hebrew; Turkish; Estonian, Finnish, Hungarian; Japanese; Chinese, Burmese; Sepedi and Basque) using a componential approach. Project brings together researchers from different countries and disciplines who have a major interest in language and emotion. GRID project was supported by the Swiss National Center of Competence in Research on Affective Sciences (SCAS), University of Geneva (Switzerland) and University of Ghent (Belgium). Here and further on the description of the project was borrowed from the participants' guidelines and from the collective monograph, which reflects results of GRID project (Components of emotional meaning. A sourcebook, 2013).

In the study native speakers judged the meaning of emotion terms in their languages, evaluating them on dimensions reflecting different components of emotional experience (Fontaine, Scherer, et al. 2007). The GRID consortium was coordinated by Klaus R. Scherer (Switzerland), Johnny R. J. Fontaine (Belgium) and Phoebe C. Ellsworth (USA).

3.1 Data mining

Before we present results of the experimental research we want to describe stages of GRID project, which we will name further on as GRID. First of all, 24 emotion terms (such as sadness, shame, guilt, compassion, love, contentment, happiness, pride, etc.), as well as the tasks to fulfill which were originally in English, were translated by the coordinators into their native languages, which we have already mentioned.

Participants of the project were asked to respond to a web questionnaire hosted on the SCAS website. In the web-based instrument each participant had to evaluate 4 out of 24 emotion words on a profile of 144 componential emotion features. The process of answering lasted from 40 minutes to about an hour. Each language had several data-gathering members (38 people) who followed the instructions provided by the senior coordinators.

The minimum necessary number of people under test in each language was 120. From the data reflected in the book based on the project results (Components of emotional meaning. A sourcebook, 2013) we see that the number of project participants varies from language to language. The largest number of people who have completed all the 17 categories of the questionnaire is 247 (Chinese, China, Beijing); large number – 220 (Spanish, Peru, Lima), 211 (Chinese, Taiwan, Chia-Yi). The smallest number of participants – 66 – was in Burmese (Burma, Myanmar) and in Hebrew – 81 – (Israel, Haifa).

We have 135 Slovak participants in the project and 125 Czech ones. Though there was no age limit, the average age of Slovak and Czech students is respectively 22.47 and 19.94. All the questions were grouped into several categories: categ. 1 ***evaluation*** (which included such items as features describing the person's evaluation or appraisal of the event – 31 items); categ. 2 ***bodily symptoms*** (features describing the bodily symptoms that tend to occur during the emotional state – 18); categ. 3 ***expression*** (features describing facial and vocal expressions and gestures, that accompany the emotion – 26); categ. 4 ***action tendencies*** (features describing tendencies to behave in certain ways that accompany the emotion – 40); categ. 5 ***subjective feeling*** (features describing the subjective experience that characterizes the emotion – 22); categ. 6 ***regulation*** (features describing ways in which the emotion can be regulated – 4); categ. 7 ***general*** (some general features of the emotion experienced – 3). These features are presented below in the tables, where they are abbreviated in such a way: categ2_i7 *felt her or his heartbeat getting faster*;

categ2_i16 *blushed*; categ3_i7 *opened her or his eyes widely*; categ5_i6 *felt at ease*. As we have mentioned above, total number of the features is 144.

Most of the participants (with the exception of people from Tunisia (Arabic, Tunis) and Peru (Spanish, Lima) and partially Ukraine (Russian, Kiev) answered questions on-line; each participant was given four different emotion terms chosen at random by the computer. For Slovak students it was naturally to be involved into the project on-line; they were called by Vrabec "generation on-line" (2010: 82). The questionnaire was anonymous, but it was necessary to mention age, sex, education, country of residence and spoken languages. It was necessary to answer all the questions of the programme, otherwise the data were not accepted. Later on all the data obtained were thoroughly processed by the latest version of SPSS Statistics ver. 21. This gave us the opportunity to capture the most important dimensions measured by GRID with a limited number of well-differentiating and cross-cultural stable features.

4 Love and hatred as emotive terms

As we have already mentioned above, there are many classifications of emotions and feelings and approaches to their study. The question arises how to process the information about them, because ways of processing of the received data are considered to be a prominent aspect of psychological research. For many decades scientists offered varied methods of diagnostics of emotional states, verbal and nonverbal ways of feelings and emotions expression. Procedures which with each coil of progress in science become more and more complicated and accomplished result from the theoretical sources offered by scholars, as well as technical possibilities in a society on the given stage of progress.

The question is how after all the person expresses one's feelings and if there are differences in various cultures on adequate perception and interpretation of emotions. As Russell claims (1991), people belonging to different cultures, are capable to perceive and estimate correctly expressions of a human face, to define on it such emotional states, as pleasure, anger, grief, fear, disgust, and surprise. On the other side there are culture specific differences in expressing human emotions and feelings.

The analysis of studies performed by psychologists and linguists, gives us an opportunity to assume, that there are universal and specific ways of emotions and feelings expression. We may speak about linguistic and extralinguistic ways (Панасенко, 2009). GRID questionnaire mainly includes extralinguistic ways, such as gesticulation, facial expression, bodily movements and some others. Linguistic ways of emotions manifestation are presented by intonational ones (categ3"***Expression*** – features describing facial and vocal expressions and gestures that accompany the emotion: spoke louder/ softer/ faster/ slower, had a trembling/ assertive voice, changed the melody of his/her speech, etc.).

Speaking about love and hatred as basic human feelings, we would like to state, that they have been investigated either by linguists or psychologists (Ильин, 2001; Fredrickson, 2001; Norman, 2005; Panasenko, 2012; Panasenko et al., 2012; Степанов, 1997; Tissari, 2003; Воркачев, 1995), but the studies were conducted mainly on a very small number of languages. We would like to mention the Edinburgh Associative Thesaurus (EAT), which is a set of word association norms showing the counts of word association as collected from subjects. According to it, love stimulated the following associations. Number of different answers is 49. Total count of all answers is 97. Here is the beginning of the list:

- HATE 32 0.33
- SEX 9 0.09
- GIRL 5 0.05
- LIFE 3 0.03
- MARRIAGE 3 0.03
- WAR 2 0.02
- AFFECTION 1 0.01

(Edinburgh Associative Thesaurus).

The list of associations shows, that top one in the list is hatred. It is a very interesting research based on English. GRID is based on a large number of languages. Its results allow us to see different ways of emotions manifestation in different cultures. Below we present results of comparative analysis of emotional markers of LOVE in Slovak and Czech.

4.1 Emotional markers of LOVE (Slovak data)

17 Slovak participants referred to these emotion terms which were described by 144 variables affording nine-point response scale for evaluation of each variable. Descriptive analysis of mean values of all variables showed, that Slo-

vaks consider the terms "love, attachment" to be perceived by members of their culture mainly through positive characteristics, like something nice and pleasant (see table 1).

number of category	description	mean
categ5_i1	was in an intense emotional state	8,55
categ3_i1	smiled	8,50
categ4_i35	wanted to be tender, sweet, and kind	8,45
categ5_i3	felt good	8,36
categ5_i2	experienced the emotional state for a long time	8,32
categ2_i12	felt warm (whole body)	8,32
categ2_i7	felt his/her heartbeat getting faster	8,27
categ2_i16	blushed	8,27
categ5_i9	felt energetic	8,18
categ4_i39	wanted to sing and dance	8,14

Table 1. List of top ten characteristics which were stated by Slovak participants as extremely common for *love markers*

Some characteristic of love markers were stated more common than the others (see table 2) (after Panasenko, Démuthová et al., 2012: 262).

category	number of feature	description	mean
features describing the person's evaluation or appraisal of the event, conscious or not	categ1_i6	that was in itself pleasant for the person (independently of its possible consequences)	7,23
	categ1_i18	of which the consequences were likely to be positive, desirable for the person him/herself	7,23
features describing the bodily symptoms that tend to occur during the emotional state	categ2_i12	felt warm (whole body)	8,32
	categ2_i7	felt his/her heartbeat getting faster	8,27
features describing facial and vocal expressions and gestures, that accompany the emotion.	categ3_i1	smiled	8,50
	categ3_i22	changed the melody of his/her speech	7,14
features describing tendencies to behave in certain ways that accompany the emotion	categ4_i35	wanted to be tender, sweet, and kind	8,45
	categ4_i39	wanted to sing and dance	8,14
features describing the subjective experience that characterizes the emotion	categ5_i1	was in an intense emotional state	8,55
	categ5_i3	felt good	8,36
features describing ways in which the emotion can be regulated	categ6_i2	showed a stronger degree of emotion than he/she actually felt	7,18
	categ6_i3	showed a weaker degree of emotion than he/she actually felt	5,41
some general features of the emotion experienced	categ7_i2	How frequently is this state generally experienced in your society	7,00
	categ7_i3	To what extent is it socially accepted to experience this emotional state in your society	7,36

Table 2. Example of the first two the most common features in each category of *love markers* in Slovak sample

People under test were of different sex. Though the number of males and females was not equal, it is possible to find out how love is being described and evaluated by men and women. Table 3 presents very interesting results of gender aspect of love evaluation and display (after Panasenko, Démuthová et al., 2012: 264).

number of category	description	mean male	mean female	sig.
categ1_i3	that was essentially unpredictable	8,00	5,76	0,025
categ1_i21	of which the consequences were likely to be negative, undesirable for somebody else	7,00	3,71	0,025
categ1_i25	with such consequences that the person would be able to live with them and adjust to them	7,20	5,00	0,025
categ2_i13	perspired, or had moist hands	4,60	7,35	0,031
categ3_i12	withdrew from people or things	5,80	2,65	0,025
categ3_i13	moved against people or things	5,80	2,47	0,019
categ3_i20	produced a short utterance	5,80	3,12	0,015
categ4_i16	lacked the motivation to do anything	5,60	3,41	0,048
categ4_i26	wanted to do damage, hit, or say something that hurts	5,20	2,12	0,006
categ4_i27	wanted to break contact with others	5,60	2,65	0,015
categ5_i8	felt negative	5,40	2,82	0,048
categ5_i9	felt energetic	7,00	8,53	0,011
categ5_i12	felt powerful	6,60	8,47	0,048

Table 3. List of characteristics that differ in Slovak sample according to gender with respect to *love markers*

Contrary to common stereotypes, men scored significantly higher in data items connected with life change – they stated that love means that they are more ready to break contact with others (categ4_i27), to withdraw from people or things (categ3_i12), to adjust to the consequences (categ1_i25), etc. more than women are. Notwithstanding gender differences in love evaluation, it is very interesting to state 7 common features which were in Slovak sample perceived identically by males and females. Love is for both genders something important in life what they head for (categ1_i10 and categ1_i11) and what they expect to get by God (or other supernatural power) (categ1_i15). They also have coincidence with some bodily symptoms (categ2_i10 – felt her or his breathing slowing down, categ3_i22 – changed the melody of her or his speech, categ3_i24 – spoke faster) (after Panasenko, Démuthová et al., 2012: 265).

4.2 Emotional markers of HATRED (Slovak data)

21 Slovak participants referred to this emotion term which was described by 144 variables affording nine-point response scale for evaluation of each variable. Description of the tables can be the same as in love markers (see tables 1 and 2).

number of category	description	mean
categ4_i37	wanted to destroy whatever was close	7,86
categ5_i1	was in an intense emotional state	7,43
categ3_i13	moved against people or things	7,33
categ2_i2	felt weak limbs	7,29
categ2_i9	felt his/her muscles tensing (whole body)	7,24
categ3_i15	spoke louder	7,19
categ4_i3	felt the urge to stop what he/she was doing	7,19
categ3_i22	changed the melody of his/her speech	7,14
categ3_i5	frowned	7,14
categ4_i26	wanted to do damage, hit, or say something that hurts	7,10

Table 4. List of top ten characteristics which were stated by Slovak participants as extremely common for *hatred markers*

category	number of feature	description	mean
features describing the person's evaluation or appraisal of the event, conscious or not	categ1_i20	of which the consequences were likely to be negative, undesirable for the person him/herself	6,95
	categ1_i27	that violated laws or socially accepted norms	6,00
features describing the bodily symptoms that tend to occur during the emotional state	categ2_i2	felt weak limbs	7,29
	categ2_i9	felt his/her muscles tensing (whole body)	7,24
features describing facial and vocal expressions and gestures, that accompany the emotion.	categ3_i13	moved against people or things	7,33
	categ3_i15	spoke louder	7,19
features describing tendencies to behave in certain ways that accompany the emotion	categ4_i37	wanted to destroy whatredver was close	7,86
	categ4_i3	felt the urge to stop what he/she was doing	7,19
features describing the subjective experience that characterizes the emotion	categ5_i1	was in an intense emotional state	7,43
	categ5_i2	experienced the emotional state for a long time	7,10
features describing ways in which the emotion can be regulated	categ6_i2	showed a stronger degree of emotion than he/she actually felt	6,43
	categ6_i1	tried to control the intensity of the emotional feeling	4,95
some general features of the emotion experienced	categ7_i1	If a speaker of your native language as spoken in your country or region uses the following emotion words to describe an emotional experience, how likely is it that he/she will be changed in a lasting way (due to the emotional experience)	4,95
	categ7_i2	How frequently is this state generally experienced in your society	4,29

Table 5. Example of the first two the most common features in each category of *hatred markers* in Slovak sample

Table 6 presents very interesting results of gender aspect of hatred evaluation and display.

number of category	description	mean male	mean female	sig.
categ1_i6	that was in itself pleasant for the person (independently of its possible consequences)	6,00	2,94	0,011
categ1_i7	that was in itself pleasant for somebody else (independently of its possible consequences)	6,00	2,75	0,008
categ1_i12	that was caused by chance	6,60	3,50	0,004
categ1_i15	that was caused by a supernatural power (e.g., God, ancestors, ghosts)	6,60	4,44	0,040
categ1_i27	that violated laws or socially accepted norms	4,80	7,56	0,015
categ3_i6	closed his/her eyes	3,00	5,69	0,032
categ4_i2	wanted the ongoing situation to last or be repeated	4,60	2,19	0,032
categ4_i12	wanted someone to be there to provide help or support	6,00	3,00	0,015
categ4_i31	wanted to tackle the situation	7,00	3,44	0,003
categ4_i33	wanted to take care of another person or cause	4,80	2,19	0,011
categ4_i34	wanted to be near or close to people or things	5,00	2,63	0,019
categ4_i35	wanted to be tender, sweet, and kind	4,80	1,25	0,015
categ5_i3	felt good	4,00	1,81	0,008
categ5_i12	felt powerful	6,20	3,44	0,032
categ5_i16	felt calm	5,20	2,06	0,008

Table 6. List of characteristics that differ in Slovak sample according to gender with respect to *hatred markers*

SPSS allows us to present obtained information in a different way. Figure 1 shows the answer distribution of the first category from Table 6. In the left column there are women's answers and in the right column those of men. We can see that the markers for hatred in male and female understanding are extremely different: men want to tackle the situation, whereas women are sure that men's behaviour violates laws or socially accepted norms.

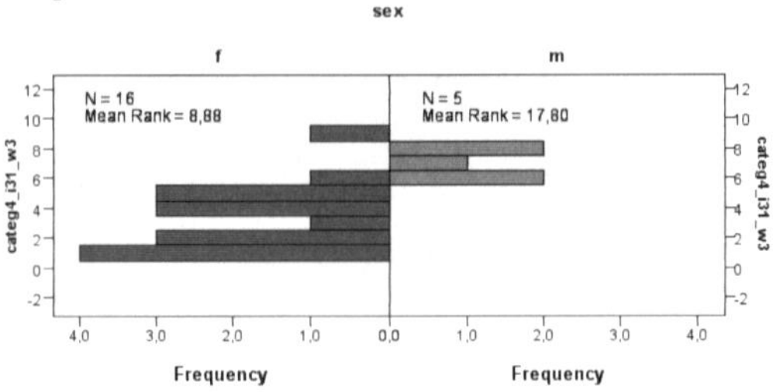

Figure 1. Answer distribution for category4_i31" (wanted to tackle the situation)

4.3 Emotional markers of LOVE (Czech data)

17 Czech participants referred to these emotion terms which were described by 144 variables affording nine-point response scale for evaluation of each variable.

number of category	description	mean
categ7_i3	to what extent is it socially accepted to experience this emotional state in your society	8,12
categ2_i7	felt his/her heartbeat getting faster	8,06
categ4_i35	wanted to be tender, sweet, and kind	7,94
categ4_i39	wanted to sing and dance	7,82
categ5_i3	felt good	7,65
categ4_i2	wanted the ongoing situation to last or be repeated	7,59
categ3_i1	smiled	7,53
categ3_i22	changed the melody of his/her speech	7,47
categ4_i33	wanted to take care of another person or cause	7,47
categ5_i9	felt energetic	7,41

Table 7. List of top ten characteristics which were stated by Czech participants as extremely common for *love markers*

In Czech sample only two characteristics (*state accepted in the society* and *felt her or his heartbeat getting faster*) scored in extreme values (mean 8,12 and 8,06); all others were perceived with central occurrence. Czechs evaluate features stated in GRID questionnaire less extremely which means they expect wide range of experiences when it comes to love. List of characteristics that were stated as the most common for "love" in Czech cultural group shows mainly positive features. They are connected with positive emotional feelings and caring tendencies (*wanted to comply to someone else's wishes, wanted to take care of another person, wanted to be tender, sweet, and kind*), and, what is more important, such a kind of the emotional behaviour is socially accepted in Czech society (after Panasenko, Démuthová et al., 2012: 266).

category	number of feature	description	mean
features describing the person's evaluation or appraisal of the event, conscious or not	categ1_i6	that was in itself pleasant for the person (independently of its possible consequences)	7,12
	categ1_i18	of which the consequences were likely to be positive, desirable for the person him/herself	7,12
features describing the bodily symptoms that tend to occur during the emotional state	categ2_i7	felt his/her heartbeat getting faster	8,06
	categ2_i1	felt shivers (in the neck, or chest)	7,18
features describing facial and vocal expressions and gestures, that accompany the emotion.	categ3_i1	smiled	7,53
	categ3_i22	changed the melody of his/her speech	7,47
features describing tendencies to behave in certain ways that accompany the emotion	categ4_i35	wanted to be tender, sweet, and kind	7,94
	categ4_i39	wanted to sing and dance	7,82
features describing the subjective experience that characterizes the emotion	categ5_i3	felt good	7,65
	categ5_i9	felt energetic	7,41
features describing ways in which the emotion can be regulated	categ6_i2	showed a stronger degree of emotion than he/she actually felt	6,76
	categ6_i1	tried to control the intensity of the emotional feeling	6,12
some general features of the emotion experienced	categ7_i3	to what extent is it socially accepted to experience this emotional state in your society	8,12
	categ7_i2	how frequently is this state generally experienced in your society	7,18

Table 8. Example of the first two the most common features in each category of *love markers* in Czech sample

Table 9 presents interesting results of gender aspect of love evaluation and display (after Panasenko, Démuthová et al., 2012: 269).

number of category	description	mean male	mean female	sig.
categ1_i5	that was inconsistent with the expectations of the person	7,20	4,25	0,027
categ1_i6	that was in itself pleasant for the person (independently of its possible consequences)	4,80	8,08	0,037
categ1_i18	of which the consequences were likely to be positive, desirable for the person him/herself	5,00	8,00	0,048
categ1_i19	of which the consequences were likely to be positive, desirable for somebody else	5,00	7,67	0,048
categ1_i20	of which the consequences were likely to be negative, undesirable for the person him/herself	6,20	2,17	0,014
categ1_i29	where the person was treated unjustly (and felt offended)	4,80	2,08	0,019
categ3_i12	withdrew from people or things	3,80	2,33	0,048
categ4_i7	wanted to be in control of the situation	6,20	3,50	0,037
categ4_i8	wanted to take initiative him/herself	6,80	4,33	0,037

Table 9. List of characteristics that differ in Czech sample according to gender with respect to *love markers*

From the data presented in Table 9 we see that for men love is perceived as something, that was inconsistent with the expectations of the person; whereas for women – as something that was in itself pleasant for the person (independently of its possible consequences) and of which the consequences were likely to be positive, desirable for the person him/herself.

4.4 Emotional markers of HATRED (Czech data)

24 Czech participants referred to these emotion terms which were described by 144 variables affording nine-point response scale for evaluation of each variable (see Tables 1 and 2).

number of category	description	mean
categ4_i37	wanted to destroy whatever was close	6,58
categ4_i19	wanted to flee	6,33
categ4_i36	wanted to run away in whatever direction	6,33
categ3_i15	spoke louder	6,33
categ5_i1	was in an intense emotional state	6,21
categ4_i26	wanted to do damage, hit, or say something that hurts	6,13
categ4_i20	wanted to keep or push things away	6,13
categ5_i18	felt bad	6,04
categ1_i29	where the person was treated unjustly (and felt offended)	6,00
categ2_i3	got pale	5,96

Table 10. List of top ten characteristics which were stated by Czech participants as extremely common for *hatred markers*

category	number of feature	description	mean
features describing the person's evaluation or appraisal of the event, conscious or not	categ1_i29	where the person was treated unjustly (and felt offended)	6,00
	categ1_i26	that was inconsistent or incongruent with the person's own standards and ideals	5,83
features describing the bodily symptoms that tend to occur during the emotional state	categ2_i3	got pale	5,96
	categ2_i1	felt shivers (in the neck, or chest)	5,92

features describing facial and vocal expressions and gestures, that accompany the emotion.	categ3_i15	spoke louder	6,33
	categ3_i17	had a trembling voice	5,63
features describing tendencies to behave in certain ways that accompany the emotion	categ4_i37	wanted to destroy whatever was close	6,58
	categ4_i19	wanted to flee	6,33
features describing the subjective experience that characterizes the emotion	categ5_i1	was in an intense emotional state	6,21
	categ5_i18	felt bad	6,04
features describing ways in which the emotion can be regulated	categ6_i2	showed a stronger degree of emotion than he/she actually felt	5,88
	categ6_i1	tried to control the intensity of the emotional feeling	5,58
some general features of the emotion experienced	categ7_i1	If a speaker of your native language as spoken in your country or region uses the following emotion words to describe an emotional experience, how likely is it that he/she will be changed in a lasting way (due to the emotional experience)	5,88
	categ7_i2	How frequently is this state generally experienced in your society	4,00

Table 11. Example of the first two most common features in each category of *hatred markers* in Czech sample

Table 12 presents interesting results of gender aspect of hatred display. According to the data, the way of displaying hatred for men is the intention to do damage, hit, or say something that hurts; whereas in female answers we find the variety of choice: to frown, to want to break contact with others and to do damage, hit, or say something that hurts (the last one coincides with men's opinion).

number of category	description	mean male	mean female	sig.
categ1_i6	that was in itself pleasant for the person (independently of its possible consequences)	4,22	1,40	0,012
categ1_i10	that was important and relevant for the person's goals or needs	3,94	2,00	0,046
categ1_i17	of which the consequences were predictable	5,11	2,60	0,046
categ1_i22	that required an immediate response	5,33	3,00	0,009
categ1_i28	where the person was at the center of attention	5,39	2,60	0,015
categ3_i1	smiled	3,67	1,40	0,030
categ3_i5	frowned	5,06	7,80	0,019
categ4_i10	wanted to hand over the initiative to someone else	4,22	2,20	0,046
categ4_i18	lacked the motivation to pay attention to what was going on	4,50	2,40	0,024
categ4_i26	wanted to do damage, hit, or say something that hurts	5,50	7,80	0,046
categ4_i27	wanted to break contact with others	5,17	7,80	0,024
categ5_i6	felt at ease	5,11	1,80	4,16E-4
categ4_i39	wanted to sing and dance	3,39	1,40	0,009
categ4_i35	wanted to be tender, sweet, and kind	4,06	1,80	0,037
categ5_i3	felt good	4,00	1,80	0,030

Table 12. List of characteristics that differ in Czech sample according to gender with respect to *hatred markers*

5 Discussion and conclusion

After the identification typical features of love and hatred in Slovak and Czech sample, we tried to identify the differences between these two nations. As we see from table 13 Czech and Slovak sample in *love markers* mainly coincide and are connected with emotional state (categ5_i1 – was in an intense emotional state and categ5_i2 – experienced the emotional state for a long time) and features regarding the bodily symptoms that tend to occur during the ensuing emotional state (categ2_i16 – blushed). As it comes from the table, to love means for Czechs and Slovaks to be in an intense emotional state. Czech and Slovaks also think that love is connected with experiencing the emotional state for a long time.

number of category	description	mean Slovak	mean Czech	sig.
categ1_i8	that was in itself unpleasant for the person (independently of its possible consequences)	4,77	2,41	0,014
categ2_i2	felt weak limbs	6,18	4,18	0,023
categ2_i11	felt his/her breathing getting faster	7,95	6,06	0,003
categ2_i13	perspired, or had moist hands	6,73	4,53	0,025
categ2_i14	sweated (whole body)	6,50	4,53	0,013
categ2_i15	felt hot (puff of heat, cheeks or chest)	7,91	5,47	0,001
categ2_i16	blushed	8,27	6,47	0,021
categ3_i2	felt his/her jaw drop	7,05	3,82	5,45E-4
categ3_i7	opened his/her eyes widely	6,45	3,29	3,40E-5
categ4_i5	felt inhibited or blocked	5,77	4,35	0,031
categ4_i14	wanted to move	6,55	3,41	9,74E-5
categ4_i20	wanted to keep or push things away	7,41	4,00	3,401-5
categ4_i25	wanted to make up for what he/she had done	5,50	3,53	0,031
categ4_i34	wanted to be near or close to people or things	7,91	5,82	0,018
categ4_i38	wanted to act, whatever action it might be	7,68	5,53	0,002
categ5_i1	was in an intense emotional state	8,55	6,59	0,017
categ5_i2	experienced the emotional state for a long time	8,32	6,59	0,010
categ5_i11	felt restless	6,59	4,24	0,001
categ5_i7	felt powerless	5,00	2,94	0,045
categ6_i3	showed a weaker degree of emotion than he/she actually felt	5,41	3,59	0,027

Table 13. List of characteristics that differ in Czech and Slovak sample of *love markers*

Table 14 shows that hatred display by Slovaks and Czechs is different.

number of category	description	mean Slovak	mean Czech	sig.
categ1_i22	that required an immediate response	6,48	4,83	0,020
categ1_i30	where the person was in danger (experienced a threat)	6,86	5,26	0,041
categ2_i2	felt weak limbs	7,29	5,00	0,001
categ2_i8	felt his/her muscles relaxing (whole body)	3,33	4,74	0,025
categ2_i9	felt his/her muscles tensing (whole body)	7,24	4,87	0,001
categ2_i13	perspired, or had moist hands	5,71	4,17	0,015
categ2_i15	felt hot (puff of heat, cheeks or chest)	6,52	4,48	0,008
categ2_i16	blushed	6,86	4,43	0,004
categ3_i4	felt his/her eyebrows go up	6,48	4,39	0,007
categ3_i5	frowned	7,14	5,65	0,035
categ3_i10	made abrupt body movements	5,71	4,13	0,047

categ3_i12	withdrew from people or things	6,24	4,61	0,040
categ3_i13	moved against people or things	7,33	5,22	0,008
categ3_i24	spoke faster	6,57	5,00	0,046
categ4_i3	felt the urge to stop what he/she was doing	7,19	5,13	0,012
categ4_i35	wanted to be tender, sweet, and kind	2,10	3,57	0,002
categ4_i39	wanted to sing and dance	1,81	2,96	0,002
categ5_i2	experienced the emotional state for a long time	7,10	5,39	0,039
categ5_i3	felt good	2,33	3,52	0,018
categ5_i5	felt submissive	2,81	5,52	0,001
categ5_i11	felt restless	6,57	4,78	0,019
categ5_i16	felt calm	2,81	4,00	0,048
categ5_i18	felt bad	4,62	6,04	0,044

Table 14. List of characteristics that differ in Czech and Slovak sample of *hatred markers*

For Slovaks hatred is associated with category 3 (***expressions***), which also includes movements and category 2 (***bodily symptoms*** – felt weak limbs; felt his/her muscles tensing (whole body). Czechs connect it with category 3 (***expressions***) – categ3_i5" – *features describing facial and vocal expressions and gestures that accompany the emotion* (frowned) and category 5 – *subjective feeling* (felt submissive, felt bad).

Figure 2 shows the answer distribution of the category 2_i2 from table 14, which has high scores in Slovak data. In the left column there are answers from Czech data and in the right column there are answers from Slovak data. We can see the differences between Slovak and Czech answers (for hatred).

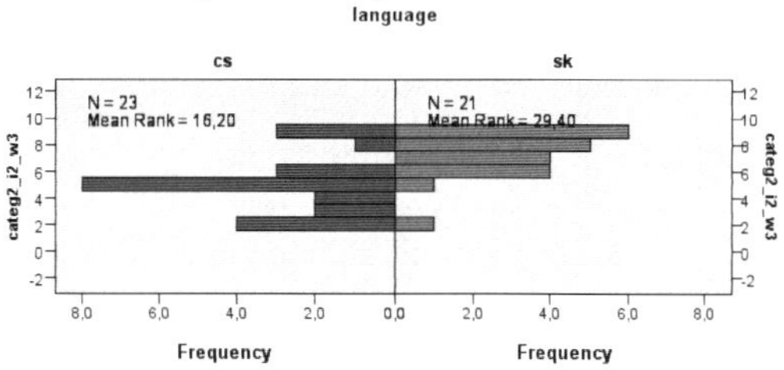

Figure 2. Answer distribution for category 2_i2" (felt weak limbs)

We have made only the first steps in the direction of emotion study in a very limited way: two emotion terms (love and hatred), two West Slavic languages, but results obtained from GRID give us opportunity to describe cross-cultural similarities and differences of the emotion terms. Experimental data show that these are two different cultures and the ways of understanding, evaluation, perceiving love, relation to a partner are different. Thanks to SPSS-based approach we can specify extralinguistic means of emotions and feeling manifestation, which are important in cross-cultural research. In general, we can compare answers of people according to their gender, age and country – characteristics which were perceived identically and in a different way; we can find top ten characteristics which were stated by Slovak and Czech participants as extremely common (ranks from 8 to 9); we can specify features of significant correlation with one of seven categories and features it includes. In particular, in Slovak GRID data we see that mainly **emotional state** prevails (wanted to be tender, sweet, and kind; was in an intense emotional state; experienced the emotional state for a long time felt good; felt energetic) as well as **bodily symptoms and movements** (felt her or his heartbeat getting faster; felt warm (whole body); wanted to sing and dance). From Czech GRID data we may speak about such prevailing features as **facial expressions and gestures** (smile), **vocal expression** (changes of speech melody), **bodily symptoms and movements** (felt her or his heartbeat getting faster; wanted to sing and dance).

As far as GRID database includes 23 languages with their regional varieties our next step will be a cross-cultural study of emotive terms in languages of different families and study of ways of expressing emotions and feelings with the help of language means, i.e., semantics, syntax and intonation.

References

Geoffrey L. Ahem and Gary E. Schwarz. 1979. Differential Lateralization for Positive and Negative Emotion. *Neuropsycholology*, 16 (6):561-571.

Components of Emotional Meaning. A Sourcebook. 2013. Johnny Fontaine, Klaus R. Scherer & Cristina Soriano (eds.). Oxford, Oxford University Press, UK.

Randolph R. Cornelius. 1996. *The science of emotion: Research and tradition in the psychology of emotions.* Englewood Cliffs, Prentice-Hall, NJ, US.

Olga Byessonova (Бессонова О.) (2009). Concepts of Emotions in the Structure of English Evaluative Thesaurus. *Studia Germanica et Romanica*, 11(1): 256-265. (in Russian).

Boris I. Dodonov (Додонов Б.И.). 1975. Classification of Emotions under the Investigation of Personality Emotional Tension. *Voprosy Psychologiyi*, 6:21-33. (in Russian).

Edinburgh Associative Thesaurus. Available at: (http://www.eat.rl.ac.uk).

Phoebe Ellsworth and Randolph M. Nesse. 2009. Evolution, Emotions, and Emotional Disorders. *American Psychologist*, 64 (2):129-39.

Otto Ewert. 1970. The Attitudinal Character of Emotion. *Feelings and Emotions. Loyola Symposium*. New York: Academic Press, US. (pp. 233-240.

Johnny Fontaine. 2008. Traditional and Multilevel Approaches in Cross-Cultural Research: An Integration of Methodological Frameworks. *Multilevel Analysis of Individuals and Cultures*. Rutledge Communication, Taylor and Francis Group, Psychology Press. (pp. 65-92).

Johnny J. Fontaine, Klaus R. Scherer, Etienne Roesch et al. 2007. The World of Emotions is not Two-Dimensional. *Psychological Science,* 18(12):1050-1057.

Barbara L. Fredrickson. 2001. The Role of Positive Emotions in Positive Psychology: The Broaden-and-build Theory of Positive Emotions. *American Psychologist*, 56(3):218-226.

Nico H. Frijda 1986. *The Emotions*. Cambridge University Press, Cambridge, UK.

Eugeny Ilyin (Ильин Е.П.). 2001. Emotions and Feelings. St. Petersburg, Piter, Russia. (in Russian).

Shinobu Kitayama, Hazel Rose Markus, Hisaya Matsumoto, June Price Tangney, (Ed.), Kurt W. Fischer (Ed.). 1995. Culture, Self, and Emotion: A Cultural Perspective on "Self-conscious" Emotions. *Self-conscious Emotions: The Psychology of Shame, Guilt, Embarrassment, and Pride*. Guilford Press, New York, US. (pp. 439-464).

Alexandr N. Louk, A. 1972. *Emotions and Feelings*. Znaniye, Moscow, Russia. (in Russian).

Milan Nakonečný. 2000. *Lidské emoce*. Academia Praha, Czech Republic. (in Czech).

Don Norman. 2005. *Emotional Design: Why We Love (or Hate). Everyday Things*. New York, Basic Books, US.

Anna Ogarkova, Nataliya Panasenko and Barbara Lewandowska-Tomaszczyk. 2013. Language Family Similarity Effect: Emotion Terms in Russian, Ukrainian, Czech, Slovak, and Polish. J. Fontaine, K.R. Scherer & C. Soriano (eds.) *Components of Emotional Meaning: A Sourcebook*. Oxford University Press, Oxford, UK. (pp. 502-506).

Andrew Ortoni, Gerald L. Clore and Allan Collins. 1988. *The Cognitive Structure of Emotions*. Cambridge University Press, Cambridge, UK.

Nataliya Panasenko. (Панасенко Н.). 2009. Linguistic and Extralinguistic Means of Expressing Feelings and Emotions in Languages with Different Structures. *Studia Germanica et Romanica*, iss. 6, 1(16):89-108. (in Russian).

Nataliya Panasenko. 2012. Linguistic Markers of Emotional Concept *Love* in Literary Texts. *US-China Foreign Language*. 10 (4):1067-1084.

Nataliya Panasenko, Slavka Démuthová, Gabriela Ručková, L'ubica Varečková. 2012. Cross-Cultural Study of Love Evaluation and Display by Slovaks and Czechs. *Humanities across the Borders*: [collection of papers / eds. Olga Byessonova and Nataliya Panasenko]. Donetsk-Trnava, DonNU, Ukraine. (pp. 253-282).

Galina I. Rozhkova. 1974. *Perception of Emotional Intonations. A Thesis for the Scholarly Degree of Candidate of Psychology*. Moscow. (in Russian).

James A. Russell. 1991. Culture and the Categorization of Emotions. *Psychological Bulletin*. 110 (3): 426-450.

Olena Sarbash. 2008. *Semantics of Positive Emotive Lexical Units: Linguocognitive and Lexicographic Aspects (based on the English, Ukrainian and Modern Greek Languages. A Thesis for the Scholarly Degree of Candidate of Linguistics*. Donetsk National University, Donetsk, Ukraine. (in Ukrainian).

Klaus R. Scherer. 2005. What are Emotions? And how can they be Measured? *Social Science Information*, 44:693-727.

Ivan Slaměník. 2005. Emotion in Social Relations. Cultural, Group, and Interpersonal Processes. *Československá psychologie*, 49, (4):381-383.

Yury S. Stepanov (Степанов Ю.С.). 1997. *Constants. Dictionary of Russian culture*. Moscow, Yazyki russkoy kultury, Russia. (in Russian).

Iva Stuchlíková. 2007. *Základy psychologie emocí*. Portál, Praha, Czech Republic. (in Czech).

Heli Tissari. 2003. *LOVEscapes. Changes in Prototypical Senses and Cognitive Metaphors since 1500*. Helsinki, Société Néophilologique, Finland.

Sergey G. Vorkachov (Воркачев С.Г.). 1995. National-cultural Specificity of Concept *LOVE* in Russian and Spanish Paremiology. *Philologicheskiye nauki*, 3:56-66.

Norbert Vrabec. 2010. Digitalni domorodci na slovensku: komunikacia a nova identita mladeže v online prostredi. (On-line generation: information, communication and digital youth participation in the information society). *Communication today,* 1:82-93. (in Slovak).

Automatic Music Mood Classification of Hindi Songs

Braja Gopal Patra
Dept. of Computer Science & Engineering,
Jadavpur University, Kolkata, India
brajagopal.cse@gmail.com

Dipankar Das
Dept. of Computer Science & Engineering,
NIT Meghalaya, India
dipankar.dipnil2005@gmail.com

Sivaji Bandyopadhyay
Dept. of Computer Science & Engineering,
Jadavpur University, Kolkata, India
sivaji_cse_ju@yahoo.com

Abstract

The popularity of internet, downloading and purchasing music from online music shops are growing dramatically. As an intimate relationship presents between music and human emotions, we often choose to listen a song that suits our mood at that instant. Thus, the automatic methods are needed to classify music by moods even from the uploaded music files in social networks. However, several studies on Music Information Retrieval (MIR) have been carried out in recent decades. In the present task, we have built a system for classifying moods of Hindi songs using different audio related features like rhythm, timber and intensity. Our dataset is composed of 230 Hindi music clips of 30 seconds that consist of five mood clusters. We have achieved an average accuracy of 51.56% for music mood classification on the above data.

1 Introduction

Music, also referred as the "language of emotion" can be categorized in terms of its emotional associations (Kim et al., 2010). Music perception is highly intertwined with both emotion and the context (Bischoff et al., 2009). Due to explosive growth of information and multimedia technologies, digital music has become widely available in different forms of digital format. Thus, the management and retrieval of such music is necessary for accessing music according to their meanings in respective songs. Nowadays, people are more interested in creating music library which allows the accessing of songs in accordance with the music moods rather than their title, artists and or genre. Thus, classifying and retrieving music with respect to emotions has become an emerging research area.

The emotional meaning of the music is subjective and it depends upon many factors including culture (Lu et al., 2006). Moreover, the mood category of a song varies depending upon several psychological conditions of the Human Beings. Representations of music mood with the psychology remain an active topic for research. Apart from such challenges, there are several computational models available for mood classification. On the other hand, the collection of the "*ground truth*" data is still an open challenge. A variety of efforts have been made towards the collecting labeled data such as listeners' survey, social tags, and data collection games (Kim et al., 2010).

In our present work, we have developed an automatic mood classifier for Hindi music. Hindi is the national language of India. Hindi songs are one of the popular categories of Indian songs and are present in Bollywood movies. Hindi songs make up 72% of the music sales in India[1]. Mainly, we have concentrated on the collection of Hindi music data annotated with five mood classes[2]. Then, a computational model has been developed to identify the moods of songs using several high and low level audio features. We have employed the decision tree classifier (J48) and achieved 51.56% of reasonable accuracy on a data set of 230 songs of five mood clusters.

[1] http://en.wikipedia.org/wiki/Music_of_India
[2] The term class and cluster are used interchangeably in this paper.

Proceedings of the 3rd Workshop on Sentiment Analysis where AI meets Psychology (SAAIP 2013), IJCNLP 2013, pages 24–28,
Nagoya, Japan, October 14, 2013.

The rest of the paper is organized in the following manner. Section 2 briefly discusses the related work available to date. Section 3 provides an overview of the data and mood taxonomy used in the present experiments while Section 4 describes the feature selection for implementing machine learning algorithm. Section 5 presents the experiments with detailed analysis of results. Finally, conclusions are drawn and future directions are presented in Section 6.

2 Related Works

Music classification has received much attention by the researchers in MIR research in the recent years. In the MIR community, Music Information Retrieval Evaluation eXchange[3](MIREX) is an annual competition on several important music information retrieval tasks since 2004. The music mood classification task was included into MIREX in the year of 2007. Many tasks were presented related to music classification such as Genre Classification, Mood classification, Artist Identification, Instrument Identification and Music Annotation etc. We have only surveyed the papers related to music mood classification.

Considerable amount of work has been done on the music mood classification based on audio, lyrics, social tags and all together or in a multi modal approach as described in (Yang et al., 2008; Bischoff et. al., 2009; Kim et al., 2010). Many tasks have been done on the English music mood classification such as lyrics (Hu et. al., 2009a; Hu et. al., 2009b), audio (Lu et al., 2006; Fu et al., 2011) and both (Laurier et al., 2008; Bischoff et al., 2009). Some of the works in Chinese music have been conducted based on audio (Liu et al., 2003) and lyrics (Yang et al., 2008).

Another issue that closely related with mood classification is to identify the appropriate taxonomy for classification. Ekman (1993) has defined six basic emotion classes such as *happy, sad, fear, surprise, anger and disgust*. However, these classes have been proposed for the image emotion classification as we cannot say a piece of music is disgust. In music psychology, our traditional approach is to describe mood using the adjective like *gloomy, pathetic and hopeful* etc. However, there is no standard taxonomy available which is acceptable to the researchers.

Russel (1980) proposed the circumplex model of affect based on the two dimensional model. These two dimensions are denoted as "pleasant-unpleasant" and "arousal-sleep". There are 28 affect words in Russel's circumplex models and are shown in Figure 1. Later on, Thayer (1989) adapted Russel's model using the two dimensional energy-stress model. Different researchers used their own taxonomies which are the subsets of Russel's taxonomy. For example, Katayose et al. (1988) used all the adjectives including *Gloomy, Urbane, Pathetic and Serious.* Yang et al., (2008) used *Contentment, Depression, Exuberance and Anxious/Frantic* as mood taxonomy. MIREX (Hu et al., 2008) has five mood clusters and each cluster has more than four sub classes.

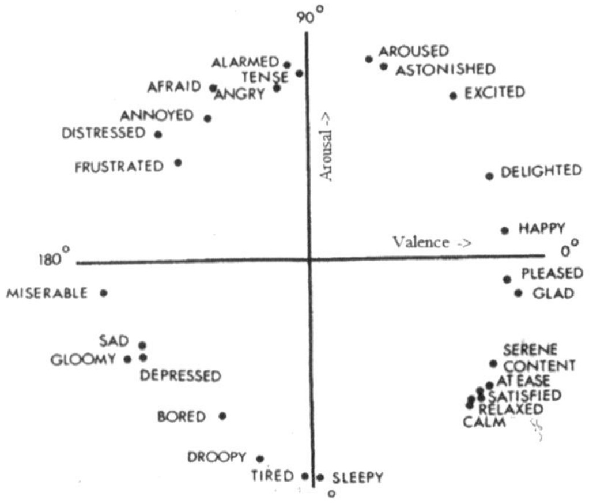

Figure 1. Russell's circumplex model of 28 affects words

To the best of our knowledge, no work has been carried out on Hindi music mood classification. However, Velankar and Sahasrabuddhe (2012) had worked on the preparation of data for Hindustani classical music mood classification. They have performed several sessions for classifying the three Indian Ragas into 13 mood classes.

3 Mood Taxonomy and Data Set

In the present task, a standard data set has been used for the mood classification task. This data has been collected manually and prepared by five human annotators. The songs used in the experiments are collected from Indian Hindi music website[4]. This collected data set includes five moods clusters of MIREX. MIREX mood cluster follows the Theyer's model (Thayer, 1989).

[3] http://www.musicir.org/mirex/wiki/MIREX_HOME

[4] http://www.songspk.name/bollywood_songs.html

Cluster1	Cluster2	Cluster3	Cluster4	Cluster5
Rowdy	Amiable/ Good natured	Literate	Witty	Volatile
Rousing		Wistful	Humorous	Fiery
Confident	Sweet	Bittersweet	Whimsical	Visceral
Boisterous	Fun	Autumnal	Wry	Aggressive
Passionate	Rollicking	Brooding	Campy	Tense/anxious
	Cheerful	Poignant	Quirky	Intense
			Silly	

Table 1. Five mood cluster of MIREX mood taxonomy

This evaluation forum provides a standard taxonomy for mood classification and many researchers have also used this mood taxonomy (Hu et al., 2008; Cyril et al., 2009). We have also used the MIREX mood taxonomy and are shown in Table 1. Each mood cluster contains five or more moods.

We have faced several problems during the annotation of music. First problem was whether it would be better to ignore the lyrics or not. In Hindi music, we have observed several songs have different music as well as different lyrics. For example, a music having high valence consists of the lyric that belongs to the sad mood class. Hu et al. (2008) prepared the data based on music only and the lyrics of the song were not considered in their work. So, we also tried to avoid the lyrics of the song as much as possible to build a *ground-truth* set.

Second problem is the time frame for a song. We have considered only the first 30 seconds of the song so as to prepare our data. In this frame, some lyrics might present for some of the songs. We have only included the songs that contain lyrics of less than 10 seconds. Finally, we have collected total 230 music tracks out of which 50 tracks were considered from each of the mood clusters except the *cluster5* that contains only 30 tracks.

4 Feature Selection

It is observed that the feature selection always plays an important role in building a good pattern classifier. Thus, we have considered the intensity, timbre and rhythm as the key features for our mood classification task. Kim et al., (2010) also found that tempo, sound level, spectrum and articulation are highly related to various emotional expressions. Different patterns of the acoustic cues are also associated with different emotional expressions. For example, exuberance is associated with fast tempo, high sound and bright timbre whereas sadness is with slow tempo, low sound and soft timbre. In our approach, we have concentrated on the features like rhythm, intensity and timbre.

Rhythm Feature: Rhythm strength, regularity and tempo are closely related with people's moods or responses (Liu et al., 2003). For example, generally, it is observed that, in *Exuberance* cluster, the rhythm is usually strong and steady; tempo is fast, whereas in *Depression* cluster is usually slow and without any distinct rhythm pattern.

Intensity Feature: Intensity is an essential feature in mood detection and is used in several research works (Lu et al., 2006; Liu et al., 2003). Intensity of the *Exuberance* cluster is high, and little in *Depression* cluster. Intensity is approximated by the signal's root mean square (RMS).

Timbre Feature: Many existing researchers have shown that mel-frequency cepstral coefficients (MFCCs), so called spectral shapes and spectral contrast are the best features for identifying the mood of music (Lu et al., 2006; Liu et al., 2003; Fu et al., 2011). In this paper, we have used both spectral shape and spectral contrast. Spectral shape includes centroid, band width, roll off and spectral flux. Spectral contrast features includes sub-band peak, sub-band velly, sub-band contrast.

Class	Features
Rhythm	Rhythm strength, regularity and tempo
Timbre	MFCCs, Spectral shape, Spectral contrast
Intensity	RMS energy

Table 2. Feature used in mood classification

All the features used in our experiments are listed in Table 2. These features are extracted using jAudio [5] toolkit. It is a music feature extraction toolkit developed in JAVA platform. The jAudio toolkit is publicly available for research purpose.

5 Experiments and Evaluation

It is obvious that in order to achieve good results, we require a huge amount of mood annotated music corpus for applying the statistical models. But, to the best of our knowledge, no mood annotated Hindi songs are available to date. Thus, we have developed the dataset by ourselves and it contains 230 songs consisting of five clusters.

The mood classification has been performed using several machine learning algorithms based on the features we discussed in Section 4. We have used the API of Weka 3.7.7.5[6] to accomplish our classification experiments. Weka is an open source data mining tool. It presents a collection of machine learning algorithms for data mining tasks. We employed several classifiers for the mood detection problem, but the Decision tree (J48) gives the best result as compared to the other classifiers.

The features are extracted using the jAudio Feature Extractor. To get the reliable accuracy, we have performed 10 fold cross validation where the data set are randomly partitioned into 80% training and 20% for testing data. The accuracies have been calculated by the Weka toolkit and are reported in Table 3. The confusion matrix of the classification accuracy is given in Table 4. We have achieved the maximum accuracy of 55.1% in *cluster 1*. It has been observed that the *cluster 5* has lowest accuracy and is about 46.7%. This cluster contains less music as compared to other clusters. The accuracies of *cluster 2, cluster 3 and cluster 4* are 52%, 50% and 54%, respectively.

We have observed that some of the instances from each of the clusters go to its neighboring cluster. For example, some songs from *cluster 2* fall under the *cluster 1* as they have similar RMS energy and tempo. It is observed that the present system achieved quite low accuracy as compared to the other existing mood classification systems for English songs (Liu et al., 2003; Lu et al., 2006) and Chinese (Yang et al.,2008) songs. But, the inclusion of additional features and the feature engineering may remove such kind of biasness and improve the results.

[5] http://sourceforge.net/projects/jmir/files/

[6] http://weka.wikispaces.com/

Class	Accuracy
Cluster 1	55.1
Cluster 2	52.0
Cluster 3	50.0
Cluster 4	54.0
Cluster 5	46.7
Average	51.56

Table 3. Accuracies of each class

Clusters	1	2	3	4	5
1	29	8	1	1	11
2	10	27	2	4	7
3	2	12	25	10	1
4	2	3	12	28	5
5	12	1	1	2	14

Table 4. Confusion matrix for the accuracy

6 Conclusion and Future Works

In this paper, we have described a preliminary approach to Hindi music mood classification that exploits simple features extracted from the audio. Three types of features are extracted from the audio, namely rhythm, intensity and timbre. MIREX mood taxonomy has been used for our experiment. We have employed the decision tree classifier (J48) for classification purpose and achieved an average accuracy of 51.56% using the 10 fold cross validation.

There are several directions for future work. One of them is to incorporate more audio features for enhancing the current results of mood classification. Later on lyrics of the song may be incorporated for multimodal mood classification. Preparing the large audio data and collecting the lyrics of those songs may be considered as the other future direction of research.

Acknowledgments

The work reported in this paper is supported by a grant from the India-Japan Cooperative Programme (DST-JST) 2009 Research project entitled "Sentiment Analysis where AI meets Psychology" funded by Department of Science and Technology (DST), Government of India.

References

Cyril Laurier, Jens Grivolla and Perfecto Herrera. 2008. Multimodal music mood classification using audio and lyrics. In *proceedings of the Seventh In-*

ternational Conference on Machine Learning and Applications (ICMLA'08). pages 688-693. IEEE.

Cyril Laurier, Mohamed Sordo and Perfecto Herrera. 2009. Mood cloud 2.0: Music mood browsing based on social networks. In *Proceedings of the 10th International Society for Music Information Conference (ISMIR 2009), Kobe, Japan.*

Dan Liu, Lie Lu and Hong-Jiang Zhang. 2003. Automatic Mood Detection from Acoustic Music Data. In *proceedings of the International Society for Music Information Retrieval Conference (ISMIR 2003).*

Haruhiro Katayose, Hasakazu Imai and Seiji Inokuchi. 1988. Sentiment extraction in music. In *proceedings of the 9th International Conference on Pattern Recognition, 1988,* pages 1083-1087. IEEE.

James A. Russell. 1980. A Circumplx Model of Affect. *Journal of Personality and Social Psychology,* 39(6):1161-1178.

Kerstin Bischoff, Claudiu S. Firan, Raluca Paiu, Wolfgang Nejdl, Cyril Laurier and Mohamed Sordo. 2009. Music Mood and Theme Classification-a Hybrid Approach. In *proceedings of the 10th International Society for Music Information Retrieval Conference (ISMIR 2009),* pages 657-662.

Lie Lu, Dan Liu and Hong-Jiang Zhang. 2006. Automatic mood detection and tracking of music audio signals. *IEEE Transactions on Audio, Speech, and Language Processing,* 14(1):5-18.

Makarand R. Velankar and Hari V. Sahasrabuddhe. 2012. A Pilot Study of Hindustani Music Sentiments. In *Proceedings of 2nd Workshop on Sentiment Analysis where AI meets Psychology (COLING-2012).* IIT Bombay, Mumbai, India, pages 91-98.

Paul Ekman. 1993. Facial expression and emotion. *American Psychologist,* 48(4):384–392.

Robert E. Thayer. 1989. The Biopsychology of Mood and Arousal. *Oxford University Press, NY.*

Soujanya Poria, Alexander Gelbukh, Amir Hussain, Sivaji Bandyopadhyay and Newton Howard. 2013. Music Genre Classification: A Semi-supervised Approach. In *Pattern Recognition*, Springer Berlin Heidelberg, pages 254-263.

Xiao Hu, J. Stephen Downie, Cyril Laurier, Mert Bay and Andreas F. Ehmann. 2008. The 2007 MIREX Audio Mood Classification Task: Lessons Learned. In *proceedings of the 9th International Society for Music Information Retrieval Conference (ISMIR 2008),* pages 462-467.

Xiao Hu, Stephen J. Downie and Andreas F. Ehmann. 2009a. Lyric text mining in music mood classification. In *proceedings of 10th International Society for Music Information Retrieval Conference (ISMIR 2009),* pages 411-416.

Yajie Hu, Xiaoou Chen and Deshun Yang. 2009b. Lyric-based Song Emotion Detection with Affective Lexicon and Fuzzy Clustering Method. In *proceedings of the 10th International Society for Music Information Retrieval Conference (ISMIR 2009),* pages 123-128.

Yi-Hsuan Yang, Chia-Chu Liu and Homer H. Chen-Yang. 2006. Music emotion classification: a fuzzy approach. In *Proceedings of the 14th annual ACM international conference on Multimedia,* pages 81-84. ACM.

Yi-Hsuan Yang, Yu-Ching Lin, Heng-Tze Cheng, I-Bin Liao, Yeh-Chin Ho and Homer H. Chen. 2008. Toward multi-modal music emotion classification. In *proceedings of the Advances in Multimedia Information Processing (PCM-2008).* Springer, Berlin Heidelberg, pages 70-79.

Youngmoo E. Kim, Erik M. Schmidt, Raymond Migneco, Brandon G. Morton, Patrick Richardson, Jeffrey Scott, Jacquelin A. Speck and Douglas Turnbull. 2010. Music emotion recognition: A state of the art review. In *proceedings of 11th International Society for Music Information Retrieval Conference (ISMIR 2010),* pages 255-266.

Zhouyu Fu, Guojun Lu, Kai Ming Ting and Dengsheng Zhang. 2011. A survey of audio-based music classification and annotation. *IEEE Transactions on Multimedia,* 13(2): 303-319.

Author Index